pocket prompts

# WATERCOLOR

Kristin Van Leuven

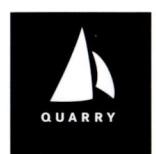

QUARRY

# CONTENTS

# INTRODUCTION

Watercolor painting can be a delightful escape, whether you're just beginning your artistic journey or are an experienced watercolorist. Yet, we all face that ever-present question: "What should I paint today?" For many, the sight of a blank page can evoke uncertainty, making those initial brushstrokes feel intimidating. This book is here to change that.

Within these pages, you'll find a treasure trove of lessons, exercises, and inspiration designed to reignite your creative spark and encourage you to pick up your brush. Some prompts are quick and straightforward—perfect for busy days— while others may nudge you out of your comfort zone, challenging you to explore new techniques and perspectives. By revisiting the basics—like painting various leaf shapes—you'll rediscover skills you may have overlooked and unlock a playful approach to your art practice.

If you're grappling with artist's block, simply flip to a random page and let it guide your creativity for the day. For those seeking a daily warm-up, we've included over sixty prompts to get your imagination flowing! No matter your artistic aspirations, *Pocket Prompts Watercolor* is an invaluable companion in your creative toolkit. Dive in, have fun, and enjoy the process of watercolor painting!

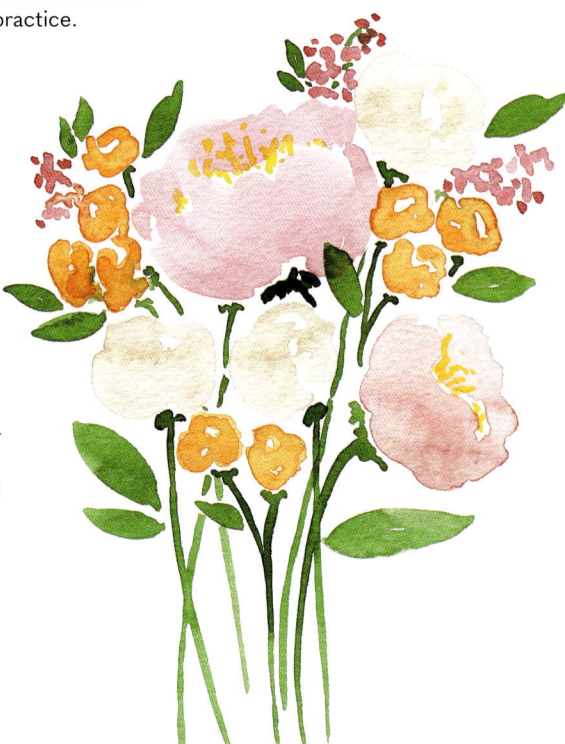

## SUPPLIES

The supplies you use are very important. The higher the quality of your supplies, the easier it will be to paint without frustration and create the look you want. The tools and materials listed here will help you start your journey as a watercolor artist.

### Brushes

The ideal brush holds water well, maintains a fine point, distributes paint easily, and returns to its shape after use.

The hair on watercolor brushes can be animal (typically sable), synthetic, or a mixture. Sable is the highest quality and performs the best; therefore, it can be expensive. Synthetic bristles are made to mimic the qualities of sable and provide a more affordable option. A combination brush contains sable and synthetic hairs to increase the performance that synthetic hair lacks while still providing affordability.

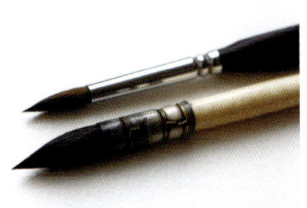 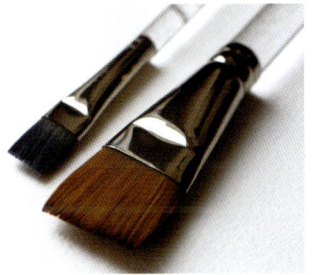 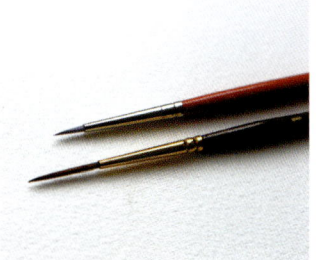

Round brushes are the most commonly used brush for watercolor because of the variety of ways they can be utilized.

Use flat brushes to create sharp lines and geometric shapes and to paint large surface areas.

Use thin, long brushes for small details, long lines, and script.

Brushes come in a range of sizes. The lower numbers (0, 2, 4, etc.) have smaller bodies, while the higher numbers (12, 14, 16, etc.) have larger bodies. The size(s) you choose will depend on the scale of your painting.

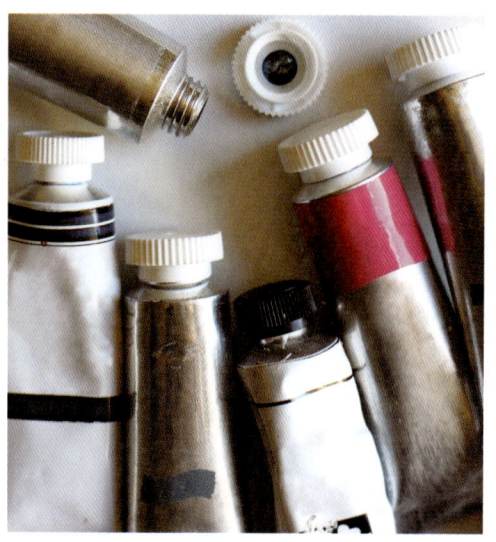

### Paint

Watercolor paint consists of two main ingredients: gum arabic (the binder) and powdered pigment (the color). Student-grade paint contains cheaper pigment and more fillers, while artist-quality paint contains superfine pigment with high permanence.

Student-grade paints are great to start with, especially if you're new to watercolor and want to practice. However, many beginners become frustrated working with student-grade paints because they can't produce highly pigmented colors, the flow is restrictive, and they fade in direct light. Aim to get the highest-quality paints you can afford, even if you buy them slowly over time. I promise you won't regret it!

### Tubes vs. Pans

Pans are more often available in student-grade quality. You can find artist-quality pans, though most professional artists use pans for painting outdoors and while traveling.

Tubes are my preferred form of watercolor. Artist-quality tubes contain plenty of paint that will last a decent amount of time—in my opinion, they are also easier to use.

### Palette

If you're working with tube paints, you'll also need a palette. Fill each well with individual colors of paint. Keep similar colors next to each other for ease of use.

## Paper

The most important thing to understand about paper is its weight. Regular printer paper will cave and buckle if water is applied. Thick watercolor paper, with enough weight, can hold water without buckling. The standard weight for watercolor paper is 140 lb.

Watercolor paper is available cold-pressed (textured), hot-pressed (smooth), and rough. Cold-pressed paper has ridges and texture, allowing it to hold more water and keep it in place. Hot-pressed paper is smooth and non-textured, requiring less water for the paint to flow easily. I use cold-pressed paper most frequently because I love the texture it provides while handling lots of water. I occasionally like to use hot-pressed paper for watercolor lettering and illustrations.

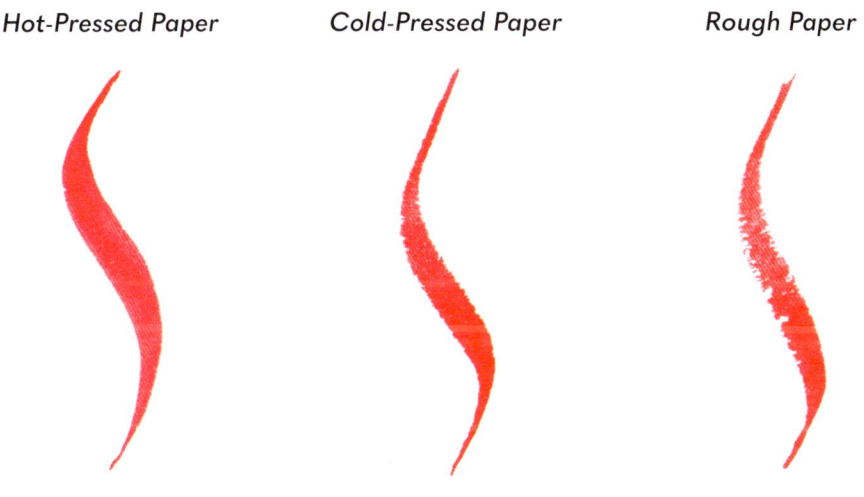

| Hot-Pressed Paper | Cold-Pressed Paper | Rough Paper |

I prefer to use 100% cotton paper because I like the way water flows on it. If the paper is not purely cotton, it can puddle in unexpected areas while painting. Some artists prefer the look of paper that is not purely cotton, so try out a few different kinds to see what you like best.

# MISCELLANEOUS SUPPLIES

Before you begin painting, gather these other useful materials.

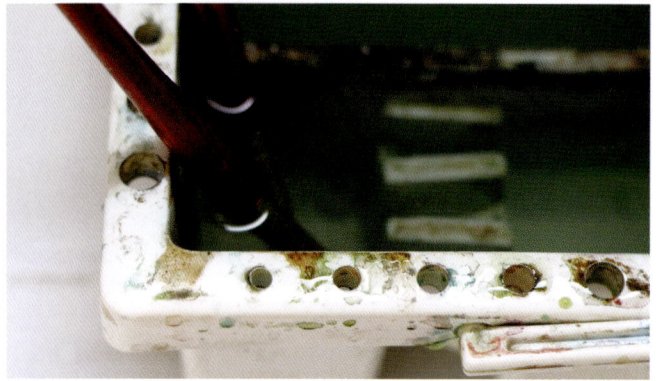

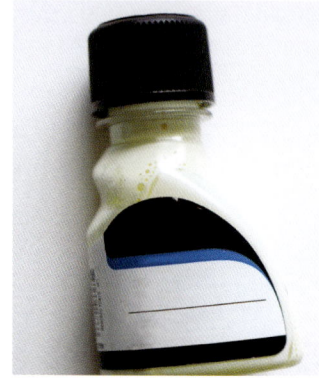

## Water

I like to use a water container with two compartments to rinse cool colors in one half and warm colors in the other. That way, the hues won't mix.

## Masking Fluid

Masking fluid protects the white of the paper from watercolor paint. You can use it to protect areas of your painting or bare paper where you don't want paint to go.

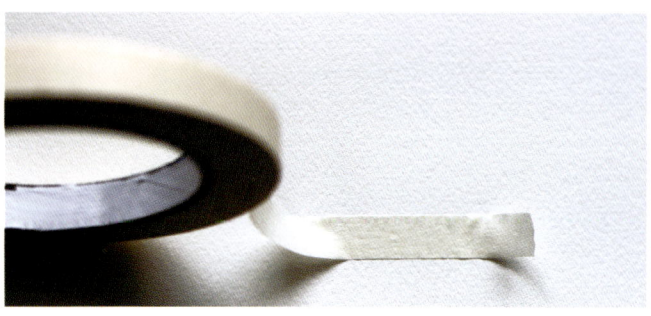

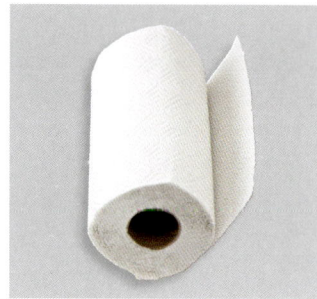

## Masking Tape

Masking tape is a great tool to have on hand for creating crisp lines while you're painting. Like masking fluid, the tape protects the paper, or dry paint on the paper, from wet watercolor paint.

## Paper Towels

Paper towels are useful not only for cleaning up your workspace and brushes but also for creating interesting textures in your watercolor paintings.

# PAINTING TECHNIQUES

Follow these tips and techniques as you explore watercolor painting. Even if you've never painted before, with a bit of practice, you'll soon become more comfortable with this fun and beautiful medium!

## Loading the Brush with Water

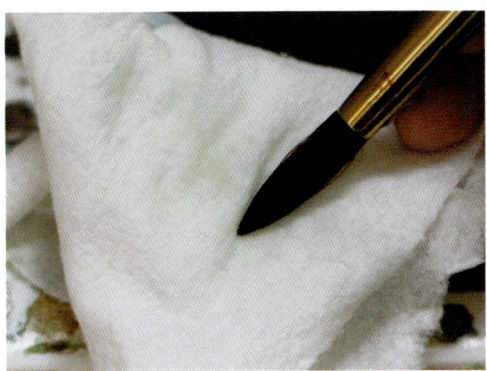

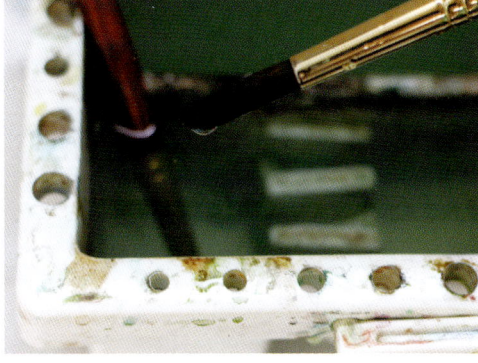

### Perfect

To fill the brush with just the right amount of water for painting, rest the bristles quickly on a paper towel after dipping in water.

### Too Wet

When you simply dip a paintbrush into your water container, it holds a great deal of water. While this is too much water for painting, it is helpful in diluting paint for lighter washes over larger areas of paper.

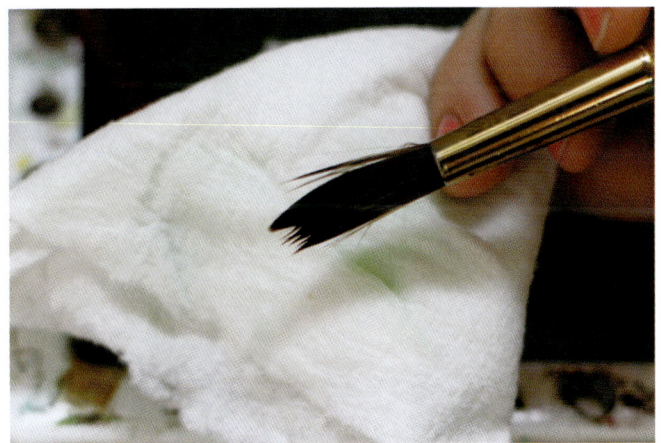

### Too Dry

If you dry the brush too much on the paper towel, it may become too dry for regular painting. However, a brush that is "too dry" can be used to create textures and intricate details.

## Loading the Brush with Paint

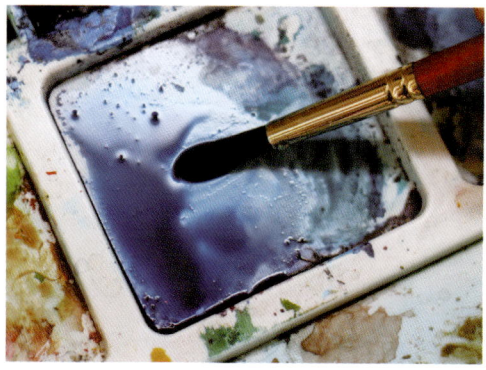

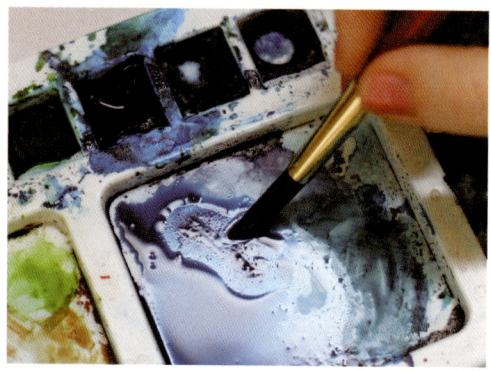

When loading your brush with paint, you want the "perfect" amount of water on the bristles. (See page 9.) Dip the paintbrush into the color you want, and use the palette to mix paint and apply more water if needed.

If the paint is very thick, the paintbrush won't flow as smoothly on the palette. For looser paint flow, dip the paintbrush in water and add it to the color to thin.

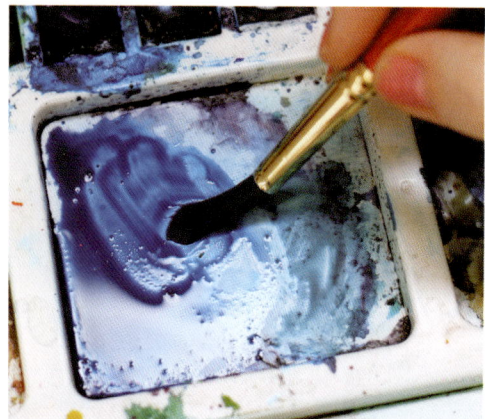

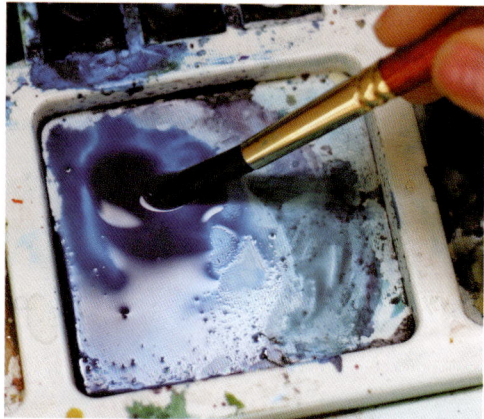

A medium amount of paint will have just the right flow without the pigment being too watered down.

Very watered-down pigment will have lots of flow and will puddle on the palette.

**If the paint on your palette is too watered down, add more paint. If it's too thick, add more water. Play around with the consistency until you find what best fits your needs and style.**

# TECHNIQUES

You can achieve a wide range of looks and textures with watercolor paint. Practice the following techniques to get comfortable with your paints and brushes, and refer to this section as you begin painting if you need a refresher on creating the look you want.

## Flat Wash

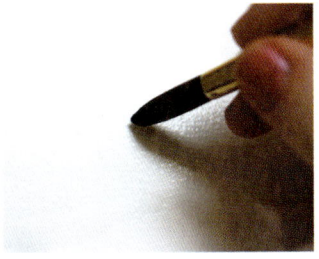 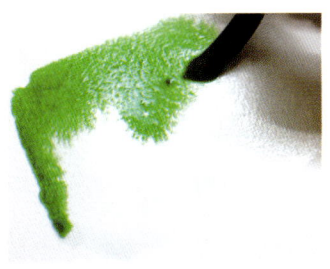 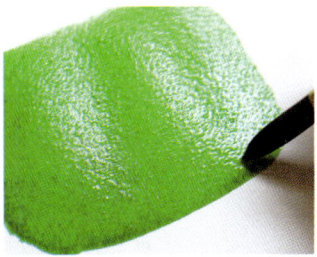

Paint the area with plain water.

Apply color evenly, allowing it to spread across the wet paper.

Avoid interfering with the wash so that it maintains the flat appearance as it dries.

## Gradated Wash

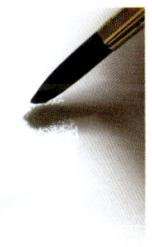 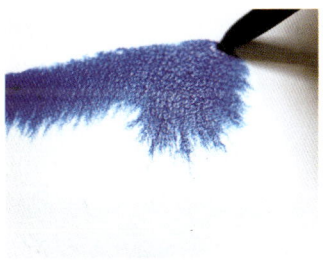 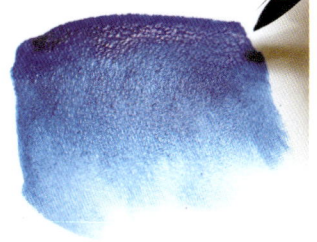

Paint the area with plain water.

Apply a heavy amount of pigment to the brush and place it at the edge of the wet area of the paper.

Allow the paint to gradually spread through the wet area so that the color is dark on one side and gets lighter as it spreads.

## Variegated Wash

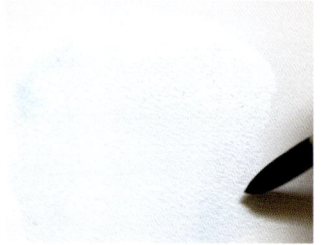 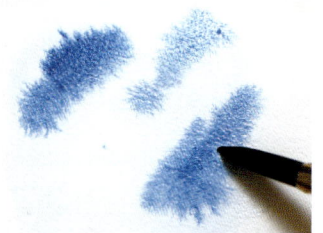 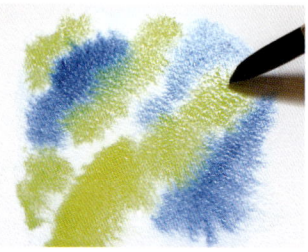

Paint the area with plain water.

Add random drops of one color, leaving white space between them.

Add drops of another color in the white space. Allow some blending, but ultimately, keep the colors true.

## Wet-on-Dry

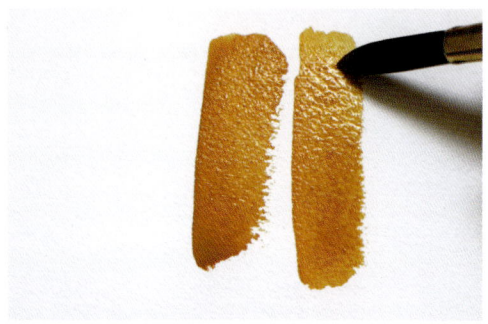

This is the most basic technique. Take a brush loaded with paint and paint directly on dry paper.

## Dry Brush

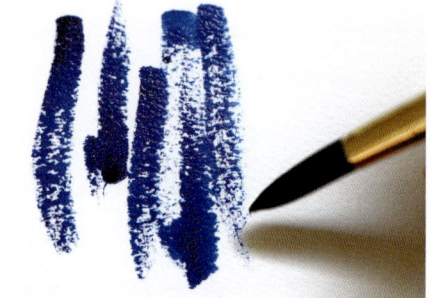

Dry a wetted brush with a paper towel before dipping it into slightly diluted paint. Apply paint to the paper, letting the dryness create lots of texture.

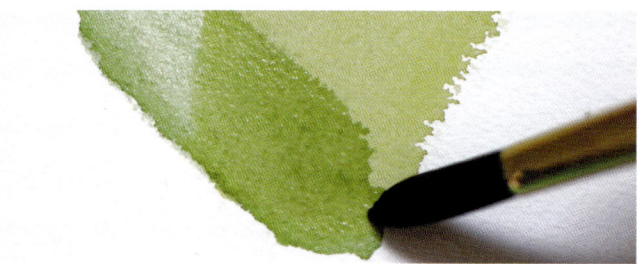

## Glazing

Apply a layer of solid watercolor. Let it dry completely, add it, and then paint another color on top of it. This technique allows you to layer watercolor paint without the colors bleeding together.

## Wet-on-Wet

## Dry-on-Wet

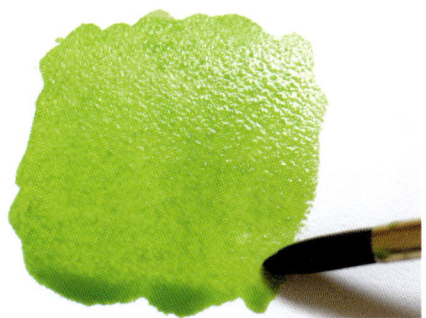

Paint an area with solid color.

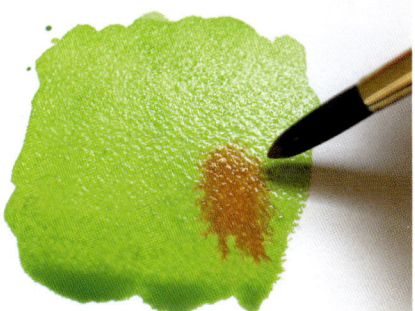

While the paint is still wet, add another color diluted with plenty of water.

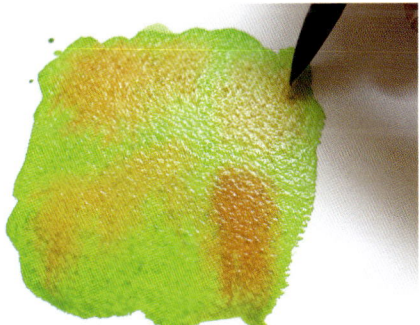

Allow the paints to bleed together while still maintaining their true colors.

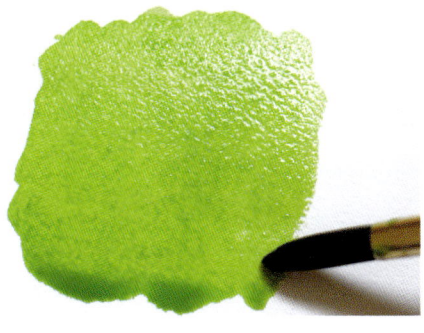

Paint an area with solid color.

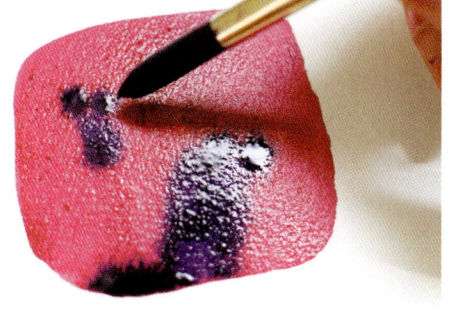

While the paint is still glistening wet, drop in another color with a dry brush.

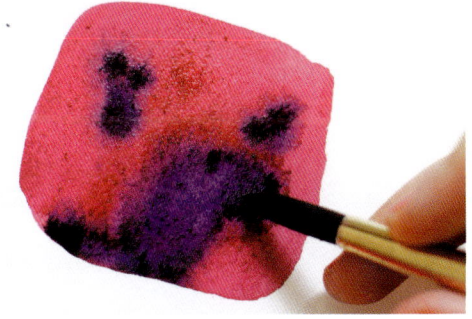

The color will bleed some, but for the most part, it will stay where you drop it and develop fuzzy edges.

## Blending

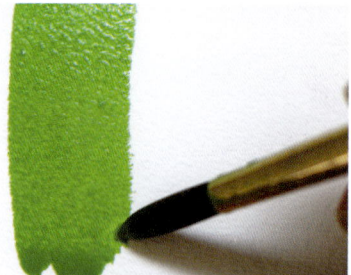

Paint an area with solid color.

While the paint is still very wet, apply a different color right next to the first, allowing the edges to touch.

This technique allows the paints to bleed into each other and mix where they meet to create a new color.

## Pressure & Lifting

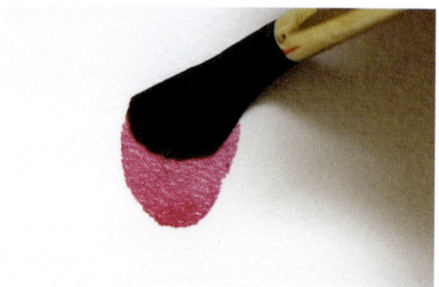

With a fully loaded brush, apply pressure to the body of the bristles on the paper.

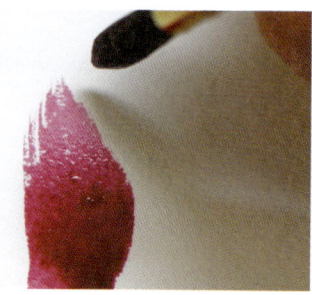

Using a quick sweeping motion, lift at the end.

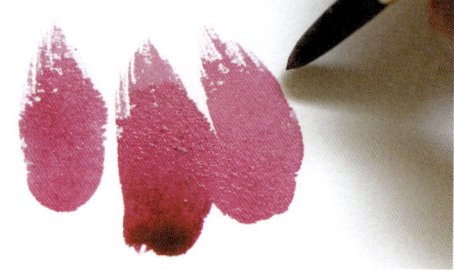

You can apply pressure and lifting as one technique or use each step as an individual painting technique.

## Hard & Soft Edges

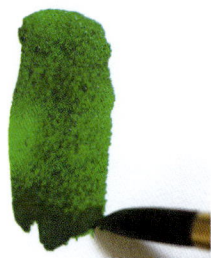 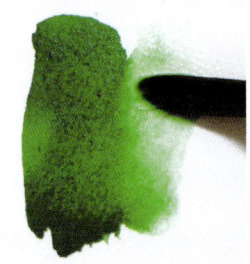 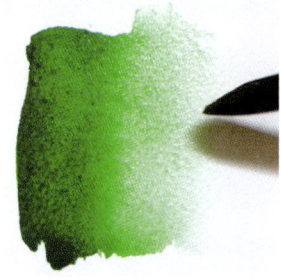

Paint an area with watercolor paint. If you let the paint dry in this stage, the edges are "hard."

For "soft edges," apply water to the edge until it blends more naturally.

The result is a subtle gradation of color that increasingly gets lighter as it moves out.

### Backruns

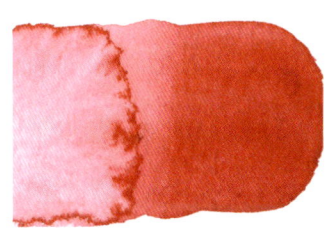

Backruns, or "blooms," create interest within washes by leaving behind flower-shaped edges where a wet wash meets a damp wash. First, stroke a wash onto your paper. Let the wash settle for a minute or so, and then stroke another wash within (or add a drop of pure water).

### Tilting

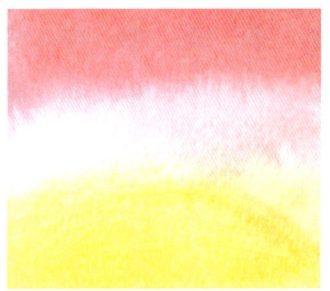

To pull colors into each other, apply two washes side by side and tilt the paper while wet so one flows into the next. This creates interesting drips and irregular edges.

### Spattering

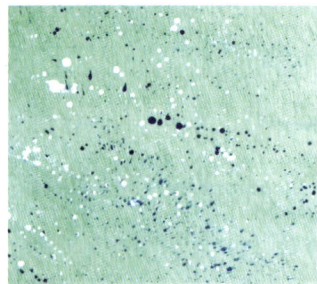

First, cover any area you don't want to spatter with a sheet of paper. Load your brush with a wet wash and tap the brush over a finger to fling droplets of paint onto the paper. You can also load your brush and then run the tip of a finger over the bristles to create a spray.

# REMOVING PAINT

Although you cannot completely "erase" paint from the page, you can use a couple of techniques to remove paint while it is still wet.

## Paper Towel

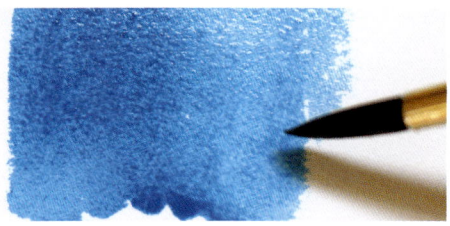

Begin by painting an area with watercolor.

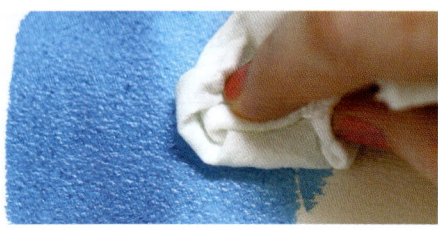

Dab a piece of paper towel lightly over the area to remove some color.

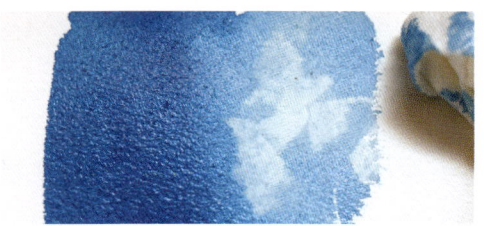

The paper towel absorbs some, but not all, of the color.

## Paintbrush

You can also sweep a dry paintbrush over the painted area.

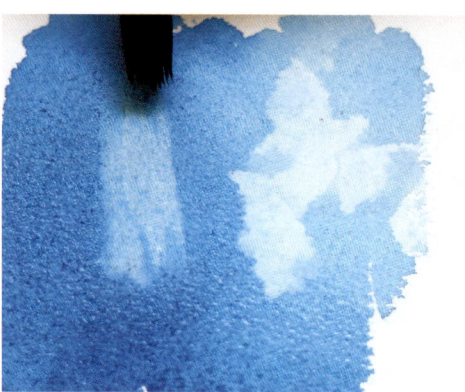

The paintbrush doesn't pick up quite as much pigment as the paper towel, leaving behind a softer, more subtle area of lifted color.

**You can use these techniques to try to correct mistakes, but they are also great tools to use as part of your painting process to create interest and texture in your artwork!**

# MARK-MAKING & BRUSHSTROKES

## *Understanding Brushstrokes*

Mark-making is the creation of shapes, textures, patterns, and lines to make art. In watercolor painting, there are many kinds of paintbrushes you can use to make marks. Each brush has a purpose and produces a different brushstroke. Let's explore some of the ways to use brushes for mark-making and the various marks brushes can make!

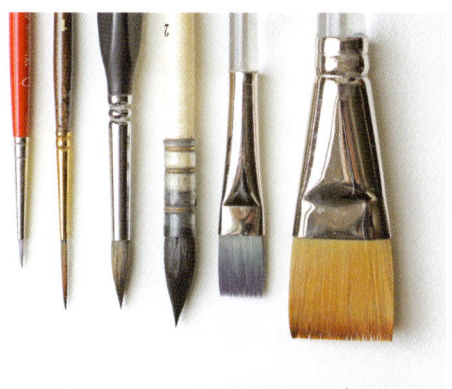

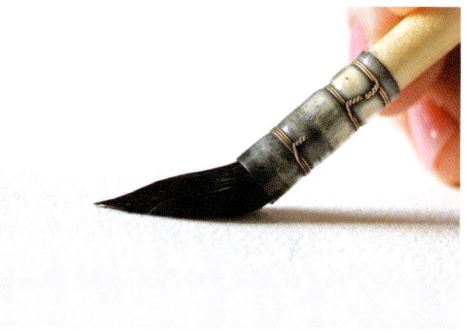

To create full brushstrokes, apply pressure on the brush to press the full body of the bristles against the paper.

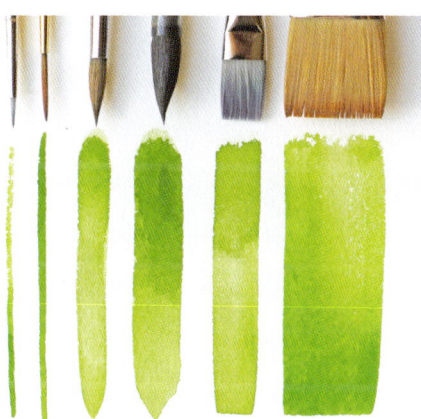

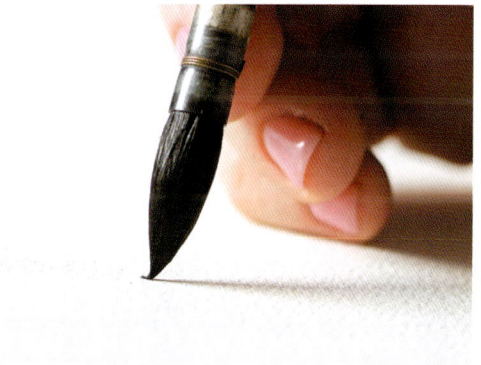

These are the brushes we'll use to explore creating brushstrokes. I use each of these brushes daily for art projects, and they can be used together for a variety of mark-making applications.

To create thin brushstrokes, apply light pressure on the brush to touch just the tip of the bristles to the paper.

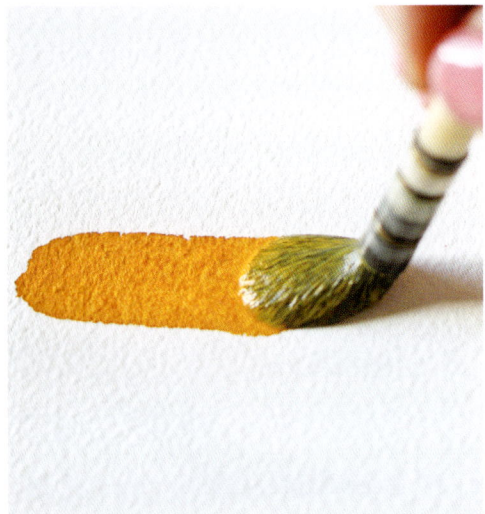

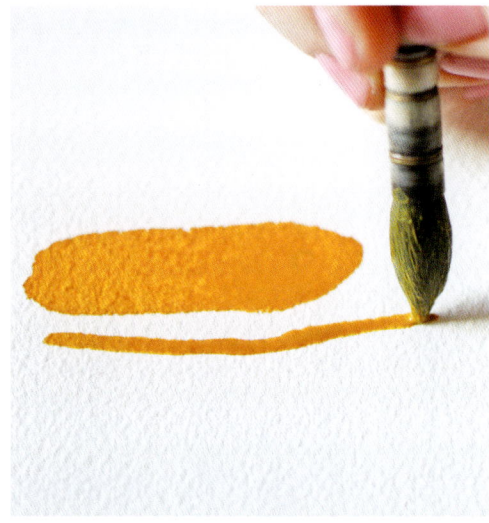

Load the mop brush with paint, and use light pressure to press the full body of the brush onto the paper. Isn't that brushstroke beautiful?

Now, using just the tip of the mop brush, apply barely any pressure to create a very thin line. The contrast between the strokes is amazing!

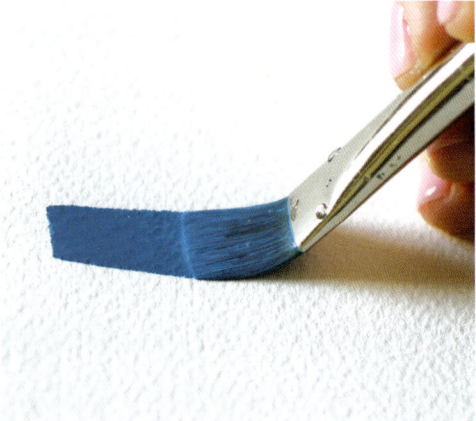

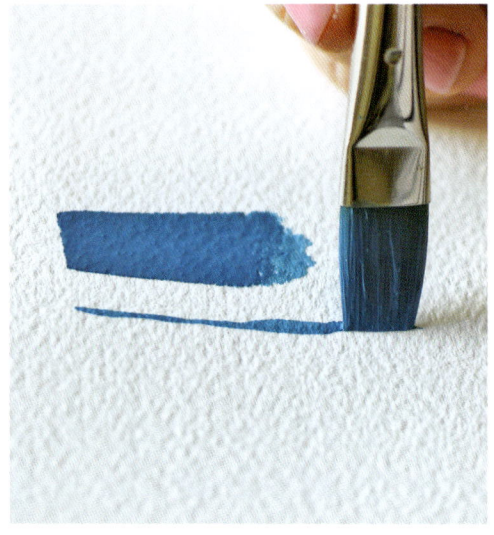

Load a flat brush with paint, and use light pressure to press the body of the brush to the paper. A flat brush makes a beautiful hard-edged stroke compared to the soft round stroke the mop brush creates.

The flat brush also creates beautiful, thin lines when you use just the bristle tip.

The way you grip the brush also has a major impact on your brushstrokes. Check out the examples below to see how adjusting your grip changes the way you use the brush.

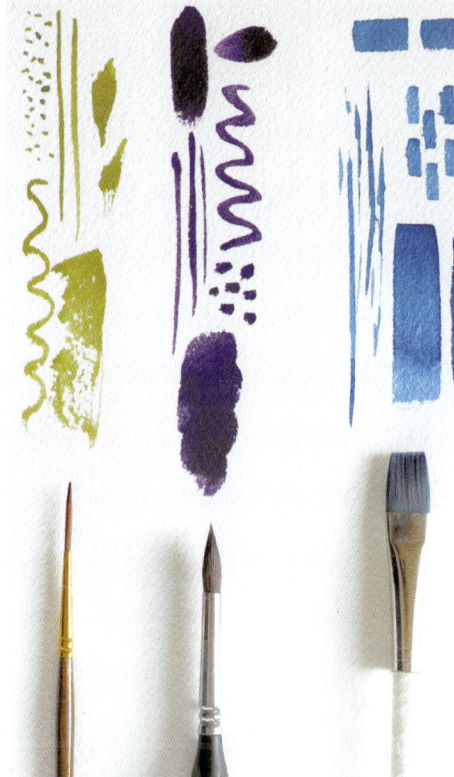

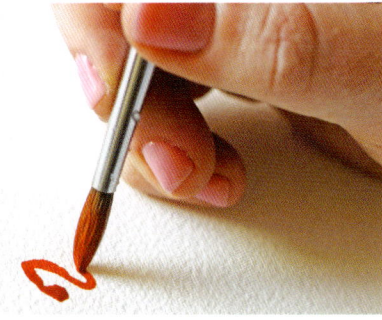

Use a low grip on the brush to paint precise details. Finger stability near the bristles gives you more control.

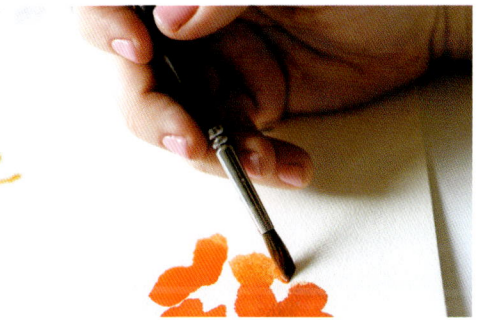

Use a higher grip to paint more freely and flowingly. This grip doesn't provide the same amount of stability and is perfect for loose painting.

**Every brush, whether you use the tip or the body, can create a wide variety of marks. In this example, I used three different brushes: a flat, a round, and a rigger. Each of these brushes can be used to make many kinds of marks. Imagine how these marks might be used in your artwork.**

**The flat brush produces geometrical and angular shapes with choppier, thin lines. The round brush creates smooth, curvy shapes with an overall sense of looseness. The rigger brush is perfect for forming long, continuous lines and can also be used for texture by applying pressure on the full body of the brush.**

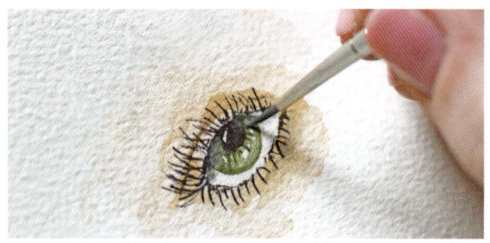

### Spotter

Use spotters and other small brushes for detail work on paintings, both large and small. Since the bristles are short, these tips don't flex easily. That stiffness is great for making small, precise lines.

### Round

I use round brushes the most because they are so versatile. You can paint anything, from loose backgrounds to lines and details to flowers, buildings, and shapes.

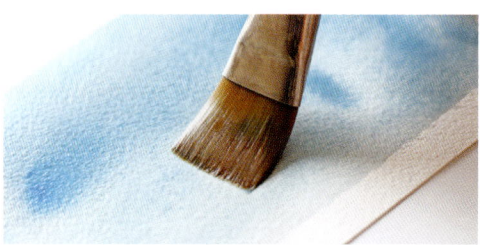

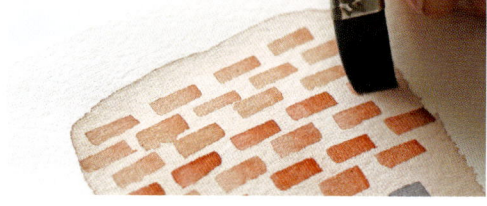

### Flat

The flat brush is perfect for creating hard lines and geometric shapes. I most often use it for doors, windows, and bricks.

### Flat Wash

I use flat wash brushes to cover large areas with paint. This is a great brush when painting the sky or laying down a base color over a large area.

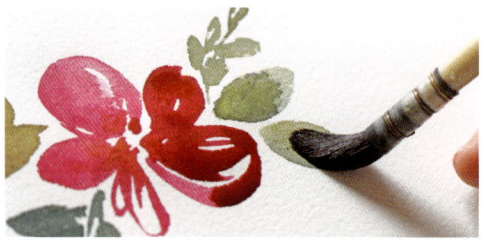

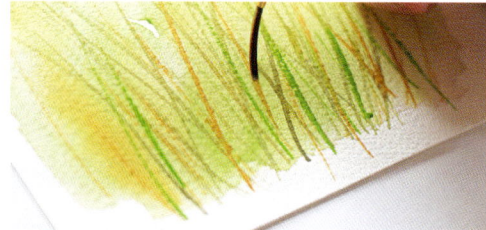

### Mop

My mop brush is probably my favorite brush. It has loose bristles that make it easy to paint free-flowing botanicals and greenery while also maintaining a sharp point for fine lines.

### Rigger

The rigger brush is perfect for long, smooth lines. The long bristles drag with looseness, making it the perfect tool for painting stems, poles, string, lines, and grass.

# EXPLORING COLOR

## *Color Theory*

Color theory is the guide by which color is mixed and organized. The color wheel is the traditional structure for organizing color into three categories: primary, secondary, and tertiary.

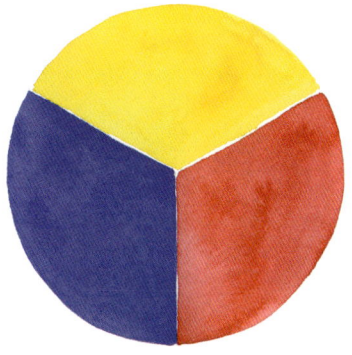

### *Primary*

The primary colors are red, yellow, and blue. These three colors cannot be created by mixing other colors. All other colors are a result of blending primary colors.

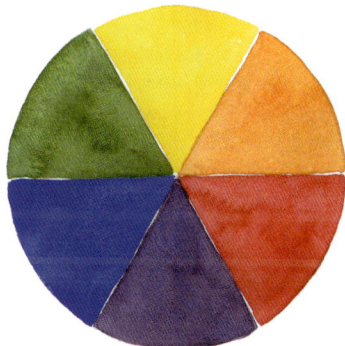

### *Secondary*

The secondary colors are green, orange, and purple. These colors are created by mixing two primary colors. Yellow + Blue = Green. Red + Yellow = Orange. Blue + Red = Purple.

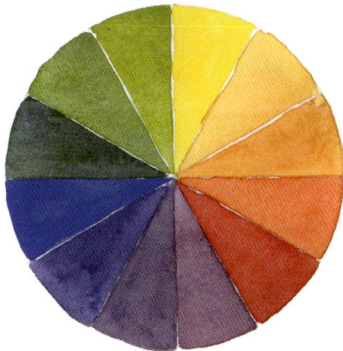

### *Tertiary*

The tertiary colors are yellow-orange, red-orange, red-purple, blue-purple, blue-green, and yellow-green. These colors are formed by combining a secondary color with a primary color.
For example: Yellow + Green = Yellow-Green.

## Color Harmony

Color harmony refers to color arrangements that are pleasing to the eye and make sense visually and artistically. When colors are used in harmony, they create balance and interest. When colors are used out of harmony, the result is visually confusing and chaotic. Your goal is to create art, using hues from the color wheel, that visually makes sense and is interesting.

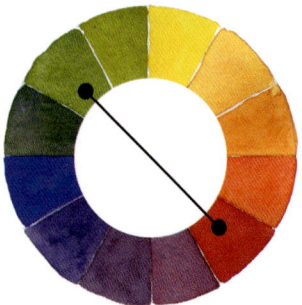

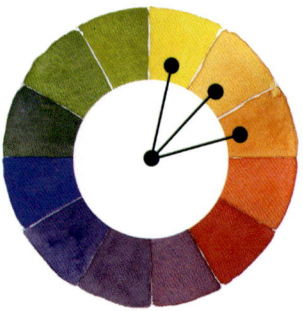

A complementary color scheme creates high contrast. While creating a very vibrant look, they must be used well to avoid overstimulation and chaos. For example, red and green are complementary, but using a softer value of red in a painting that uses this color scheme will avoid visual confusion.

Analogous colors are any three colors that are side by side on the color wheel. For example, yellow, yellow-orange, and orange. Colors next to each other on the color wheel blend easily together, so they make sense to the brain. One color usually dominates.

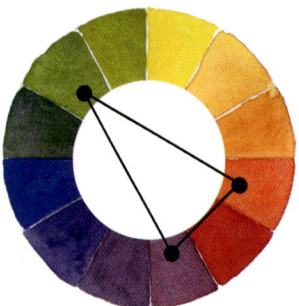

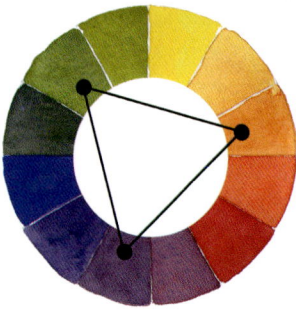

This is an adaptation of the complementary color scheme. The use of these colors produces high contrast with less conflict. For example, green, red-purple, and red-orange.

An arrangement of triadic colors creates high contrast, even when using lighter color values. This combination is very vibrant, and usually, one color dominates while the other two support.

## Triadic

Color mixing is the process of combining colors to create a new color. Learning to mix your colors to make the right hue is an important skill you'll use for every project. There are three ways you can mix color: on the paper, on the palette, and by glazing.

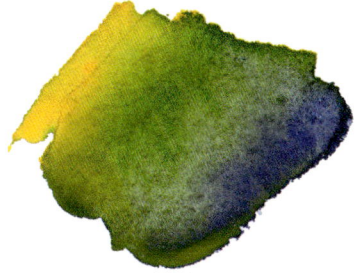

### Paper

If you're okay with the primary colors not being completely blended, you can mix colors right on watercolor paper. Typically, this approach isn't completely even. In this example, I have mixed green, but note how some places look yellower or bluer.

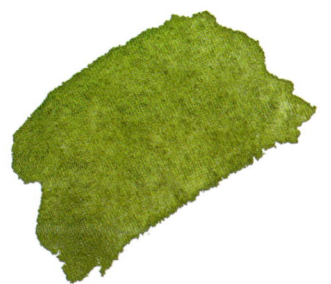

### Palette

To create an even and consistent color, mix colors on your palette before dropping them onto the paper. With this technique, you can completely control the color balance before applying it to paper.

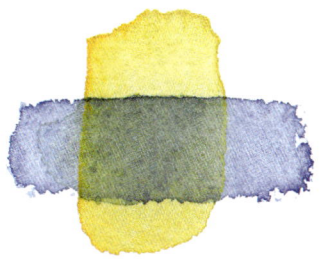

### Glazing

Glazing is a method of applying layers of watercolor over each other. This is a great way to create the color you want but also add dimension with glimpses of the colors underneath.

## Color Mixing Chart

It's important to know not only how to mix other colors from primary colors but also how to mix the specific paint colors on your palette. Most watercolor artists have a wide variety of colors on their palette, not just the primaries. It's very valuable to make a chart of all the different hue combinations your paints can create. This is my most used tool, and I refer to it daily. Follow these tips to create your own.

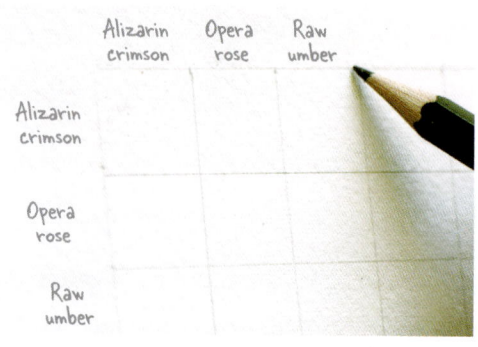

Using a ruler, chart and draw squares based on the number of paints you will use in your chart. I used eight colors, which makes sixty-four squares. Then, write the names of the colors you will be using along the left side and the top in the same order.

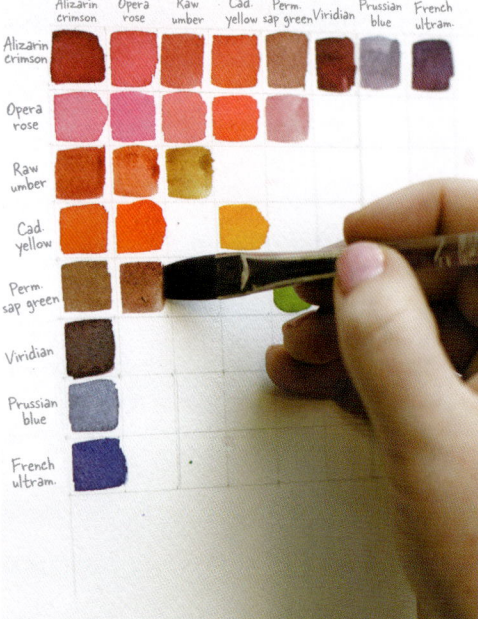

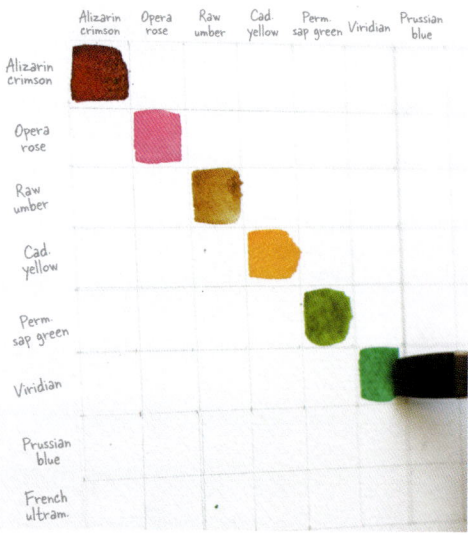

The middle diagonal line is the "pure color," where the name of the paint is the same on the side and top. I paint this row first.

There will be two places on the chart where the same color combination meets. Remember: the color listed on the left is the dominant color. Use that color as the base, and add a little of the color listed at the top to create the hue for each square.

I like to mix both color combos at the same time to save paint. For example, when the dominant color is opera rose, and the additive color is viridian, I add a little viridian to opera rose on my palette and then place that color in its square. Next, I take that paint mixture and add viridian until it becomes the dominant color. Then, I drop that color into its square.

Isn't the chart amazing? You can see all the different colors that can be created with your palette, and you may even find some combinations that pleasantly surprise you!

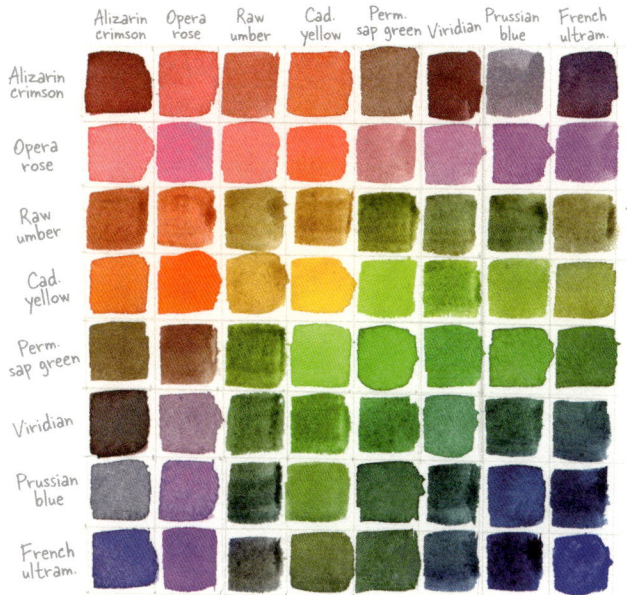

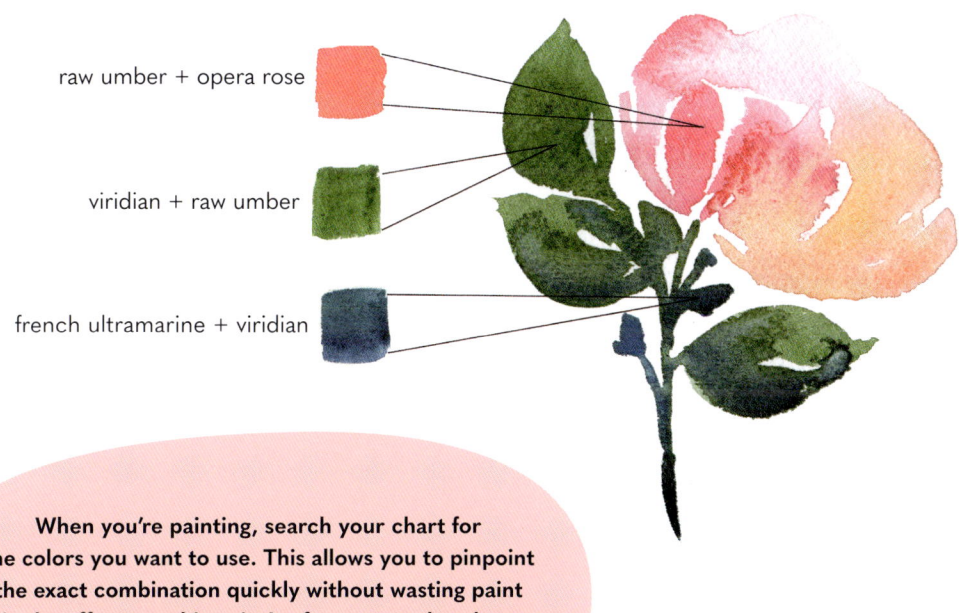

raw umber + opera rose

viridian + raw umber

french ultramarine + viridian

When you're painting, search your chart for the colors you want to use. This allows you to pinpoint the exact combination quickly without wasting paint in the effort to achieve it. I refer to my color chart daily to help me mix the perfect hues.

# VALUE

Value is the relative lightness or darkness of a color. To make a color value lighter, add water. To make a color value darker, add pigment.

To explore the color variations within a combo, as well as their value, create a smaller mixing chart. Paint the top and bottom rows with 100% unmixed color, the middle row with a 50/50 mix, and the other two rows with more of the pure color each row is closest to.

QUINACRIDONE GOLD 100%

QG 75% - V 25%

QG 50% - V 50%

V 75% - QG 25%

VIRIDIAN 100%

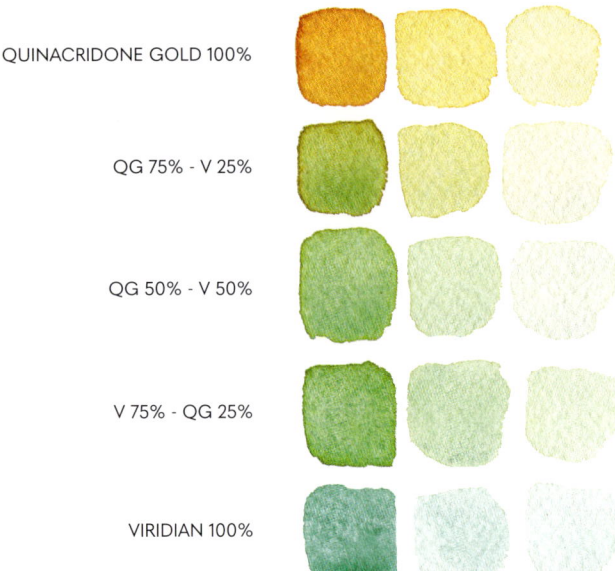

Example: Place quinacridone gold at the top and viridian at the bottom. Mix both together to create an even mixture for the middle row. For the row closest to quinacridone gold, add more yellow. For the row closest to viridian, add more green. Add water to the colors to create the lighter values in the chart.

To help determine the value of a color, compare it to the gray scale. The gray scale helps you determine which shade is closest in value to your color. For example, yellow matches up with the lighter values of gray, and purple matches up with the darker values. When painting, values are an important part of making the overall piece make sense.

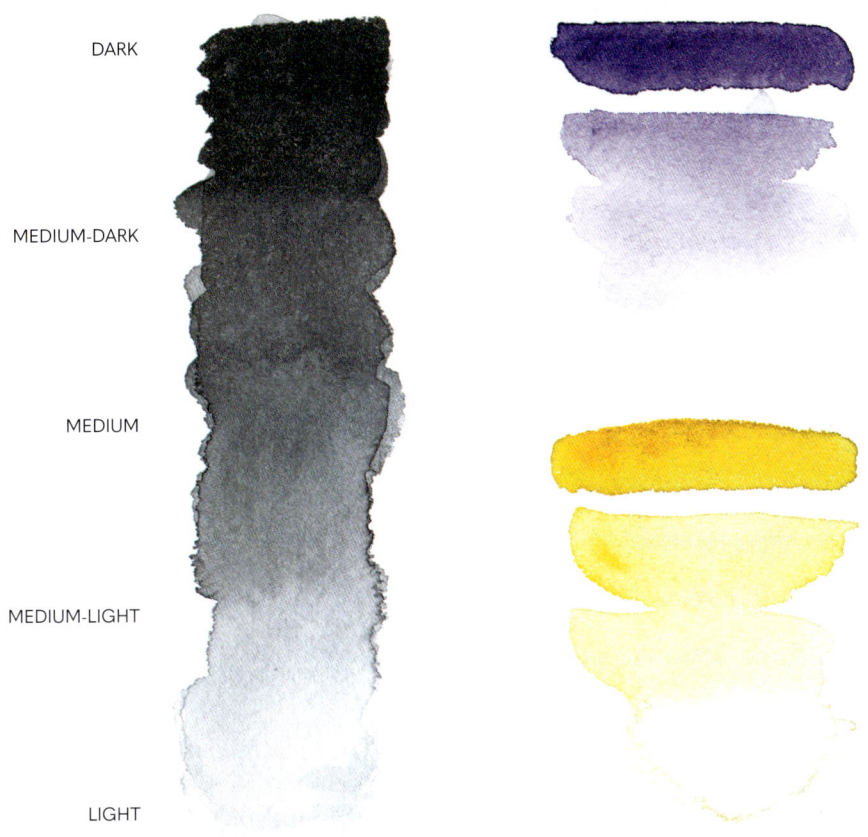

DARK

MEDIUM-DARK

MEDIUM

MEDIUM-LIGHT

LIGHT

There are five basic values: dark, medium-dark, medium, medium-light, and light. Values are easier to see in gray scale. It's important to train your eye to see the values in color so that your paintings look accurate.

You can change the value of a color by either lightening it with water or darkening it with pigment.

## Painting in Black & White

Painting in black and white not only helps you practice and learn how to understand color values, but it also creates a pretty, monochrome aesthetic.

Using different values of black, I can create a monochrome painting with depth and dimension.

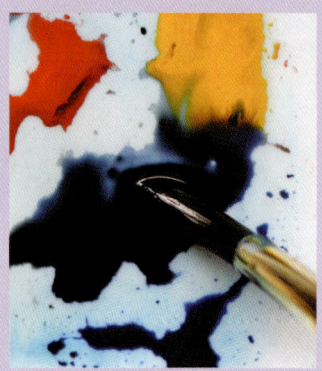

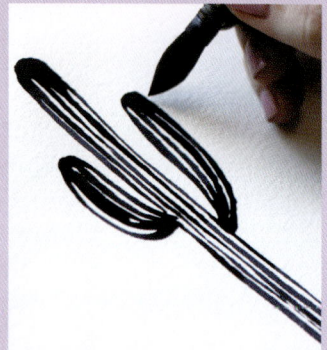

Use your color mixing skills to create black by mixing all three primary colors until you find the hue you want. This mixing technique produces more dimension with blue, red, and yellow undertones.

Use the white of the paper as much as possible. It's hard to add white back into a painting, so you must either paint around the areas you want to keep white or use masking fluid.

White watercolor, if used at all, should be used sparingly or only for certain techniques. A perfect instance of when to use white paint is when you want a color to be opaque or less see-through. You can add white to any color to achieve this, and adding it to black hues creates lovely, opaque, cloudy grays.

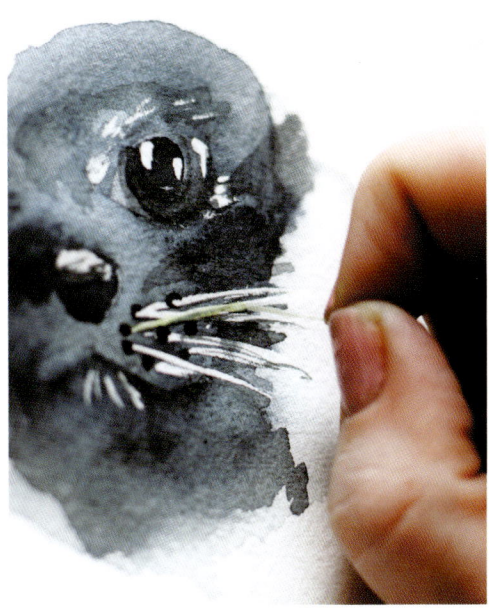

Use masking fluid (see page 42) to maintain perfect whites while using other hues freely.

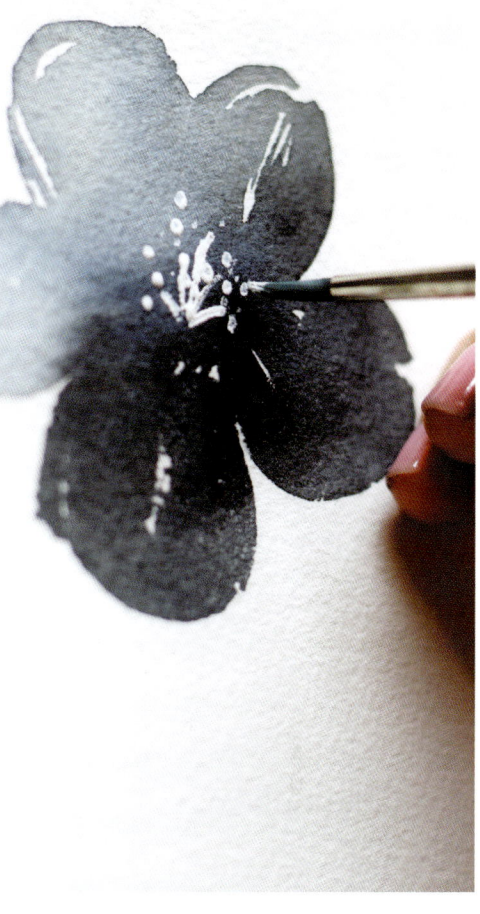

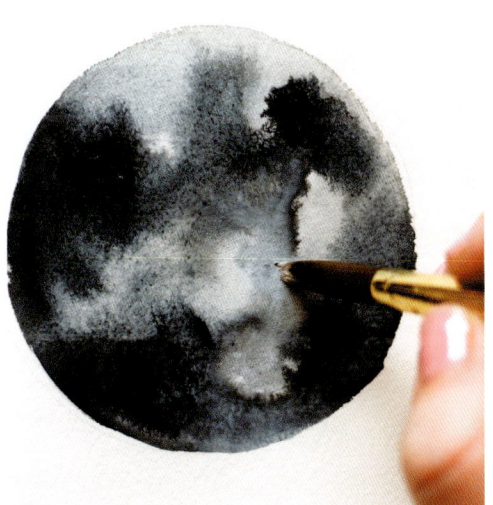

Use white watercolor straight from the tube, without adding water, to apply smaller details.

White watercolor helps make the perfect opaque gray for this moon.

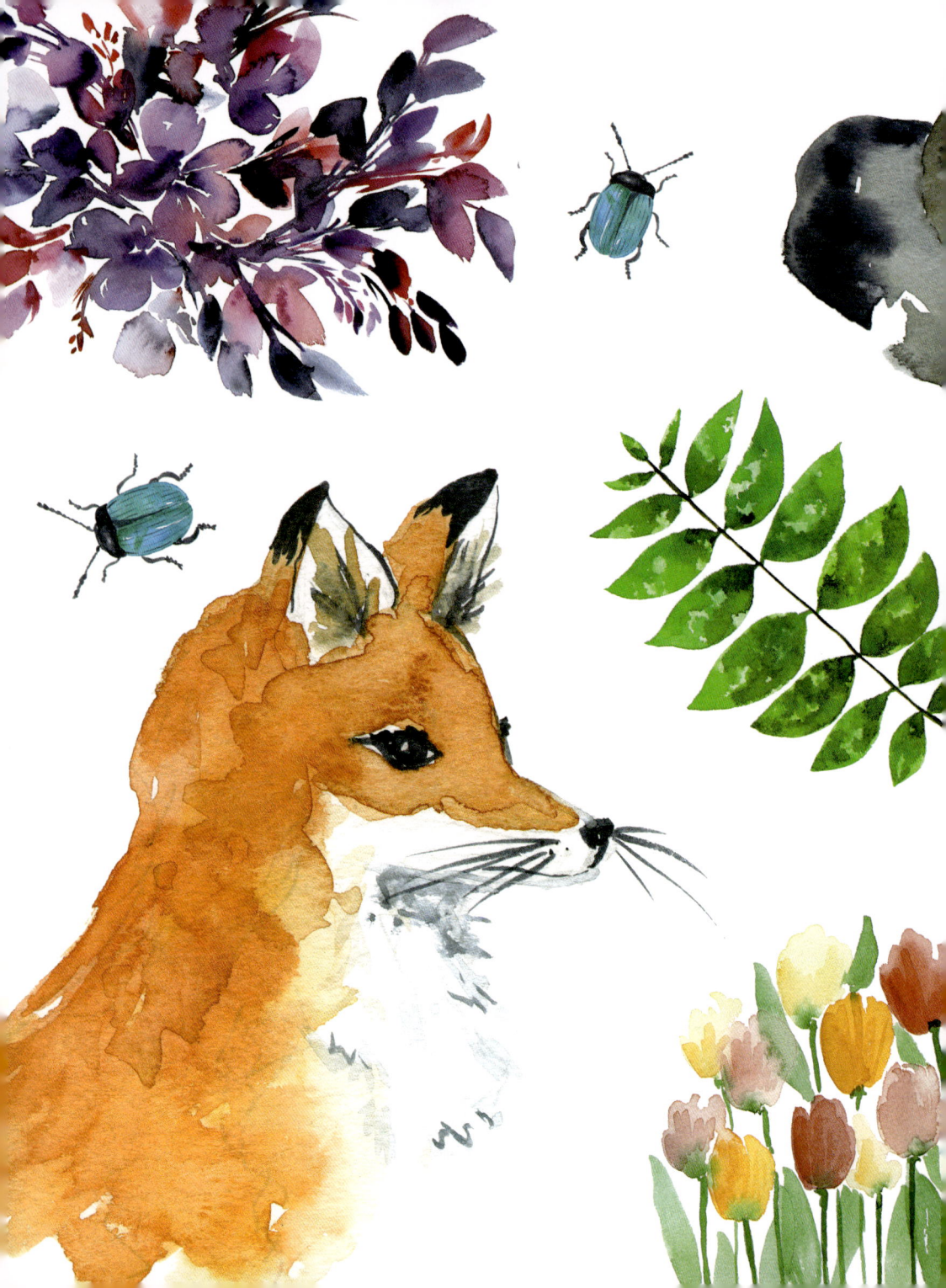

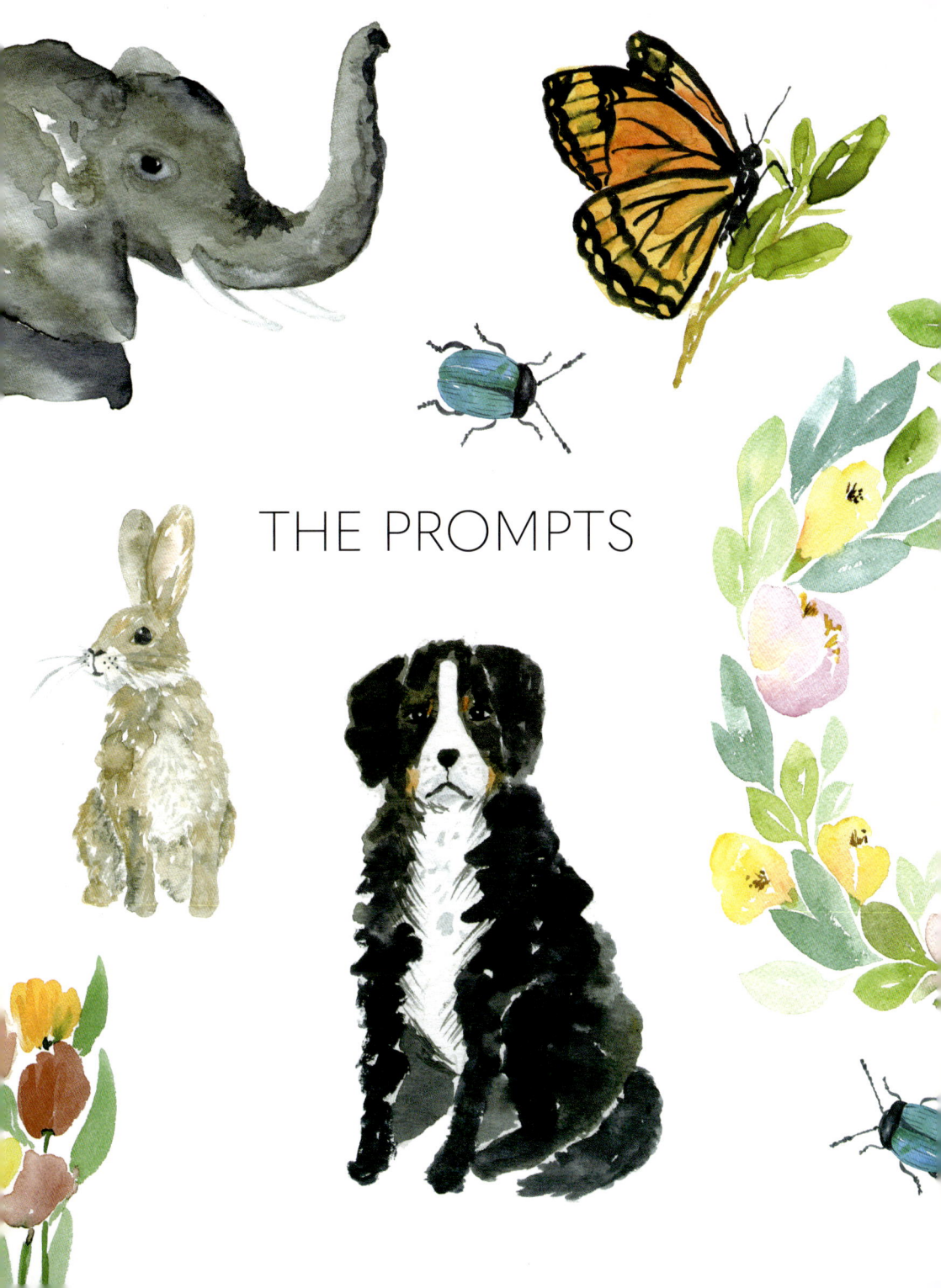

# THE PROMPTS

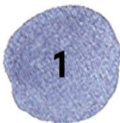

# 1 PAINT CIRCLES & OVALS

*Circles and ovals seem basic, but they can be tricky to master. I find it easiest to paint the outline first and then fill it in with a round brush.*

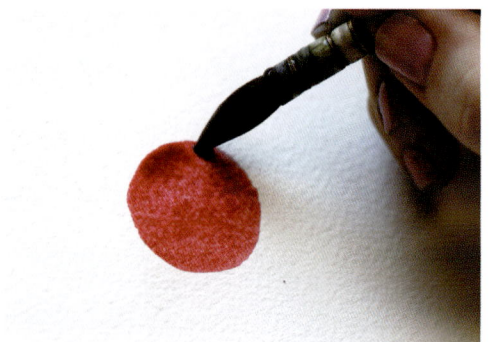

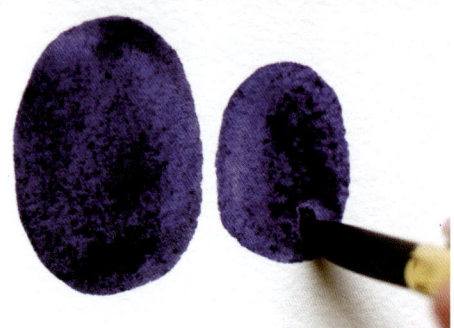

With a little practice, you'll find that you can paint near-perfect circles.

Circles and ovals are found everywhere in patterns and nature. Having a basic knowledge of these shapes will give you the foundation needed to paint them in real-life pieces.

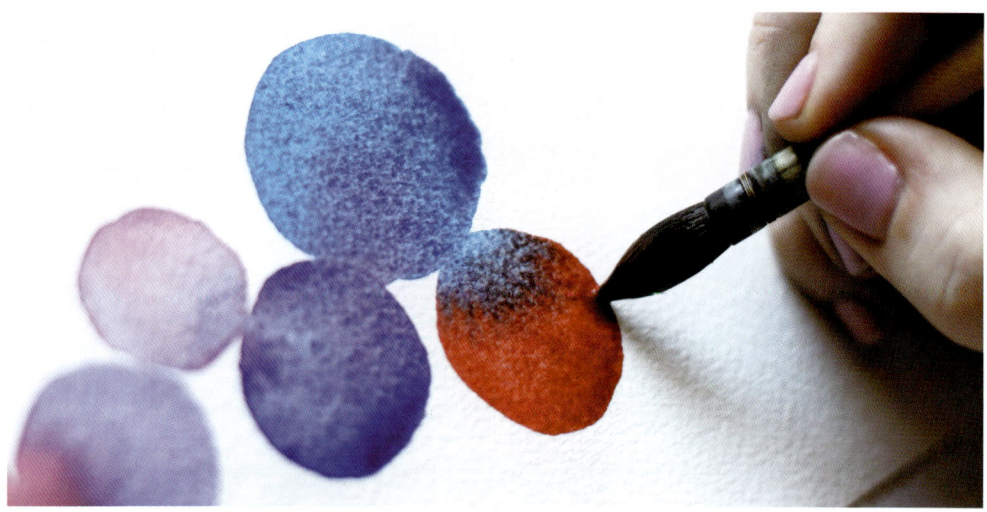

Try painting circles to warm up before beginning a new painting or to get familiar with a new paintbrush.

# PAINT TRIANGLES & DIAMONDS

*Triangles and diamonds may be more angular than circles, but they are also easier to paint if you draw the outline of the shape first and then fill it in.*

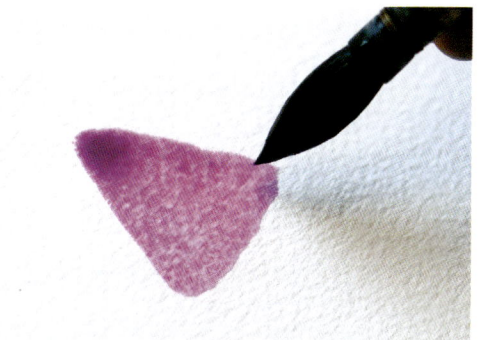

Use a round brush to paint triangles and diamonds.

Triangles and diamonds are common shapes in geometric patterns and in more structured objects, such as buildings.

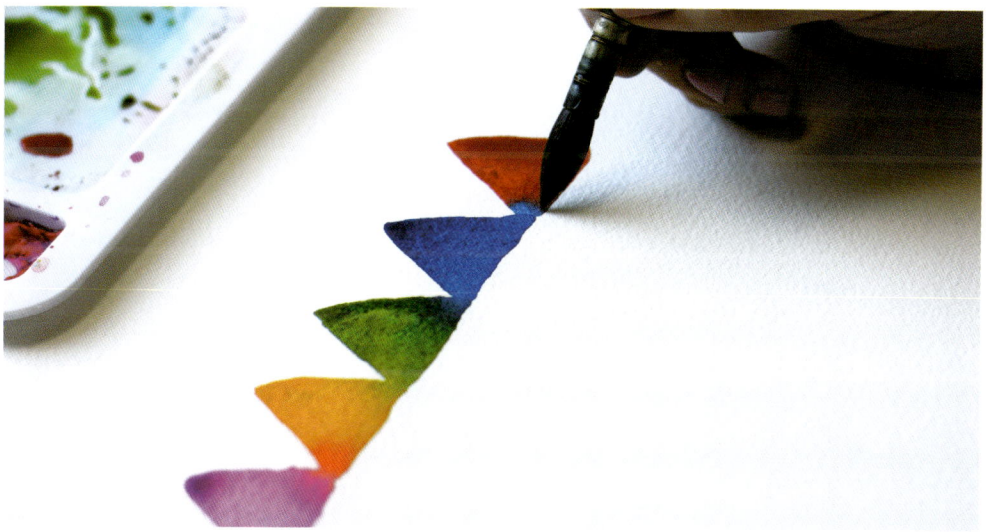

Paint triangles to practice painting straight, crisp lines with your round brushes.

# 3 PAINT SQUARES & RECTANGLES

*It's easy to form squares and rectangles with a flat brush. Short strokes make squares, and longer strokes make rectangles. You can also use a round brush to draw the outline of the shape and fill it in.*

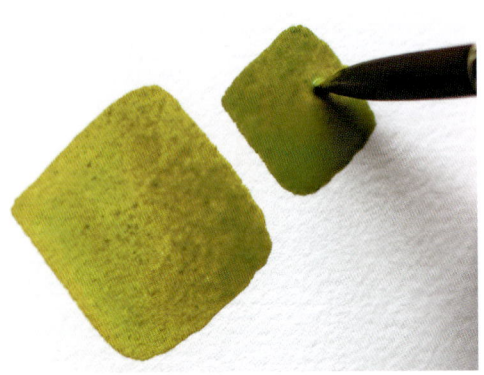 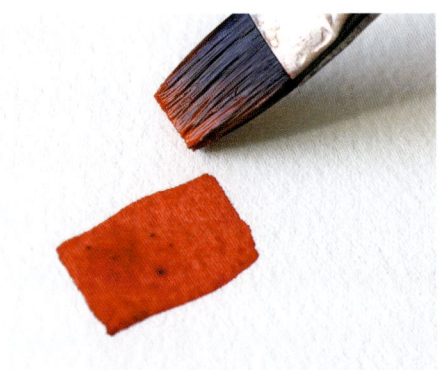

Using a round brush will produce softer corners.   A flat brush will produce sharper corners.

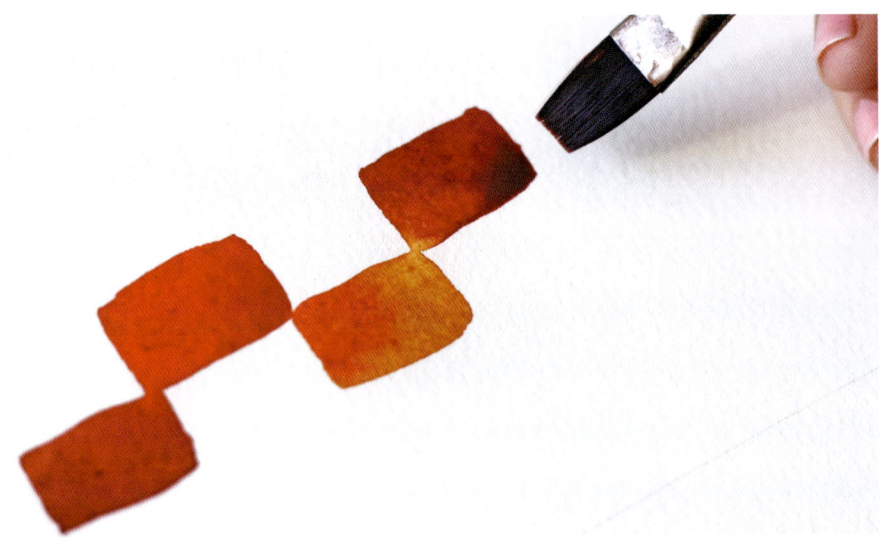

Squares and rectangles are very uniform. You can spot these geometric shapes in all kinds of structures, buildings, and even in nature.

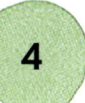

# 4 EXPERIMENT WITH PAINTING OTHER SHAPES

*Other shapes, such as hearts, stars, and abstract shapes, are fun to paint—and they are open-ended for unique approaches and interpretation.*

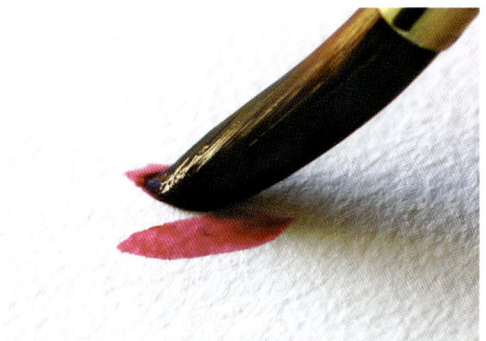

Paint hearts by pressing down on a round brush to create each arch.

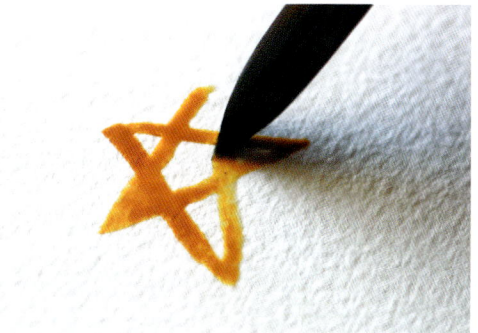

Stars are hard to form freehand, so I suggest creating a crisscross star and filling it in for a more uniform look.

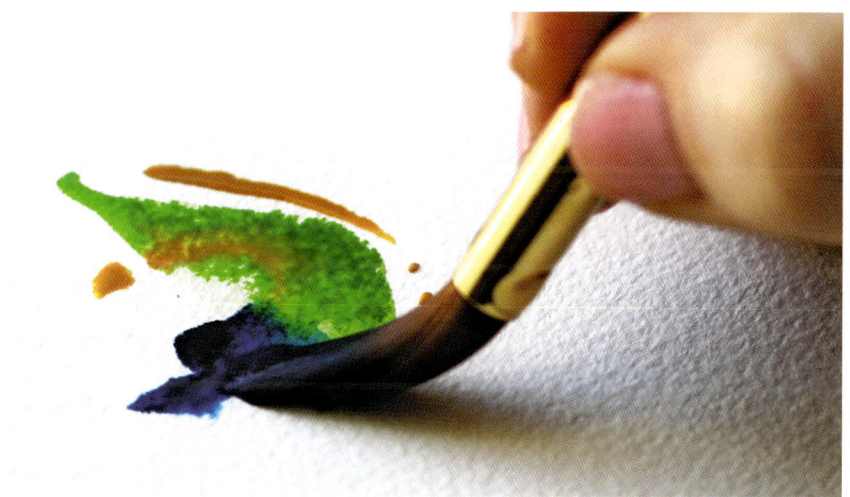

Anything goes when painting abstract shapes. Dots, lines, ovals, drops—whatever inspires you to create. Although abstract can be seen as "random," a lot of thought should go into the placement and flow of each shape.

# CREATE ALLOVER PATTERNS

*To take your skills to the next level, try creating some allover patterns using all the different shapes. You can combine shapes for a fun mixed pattern or stick to one or two shapes for a more consistent look.*

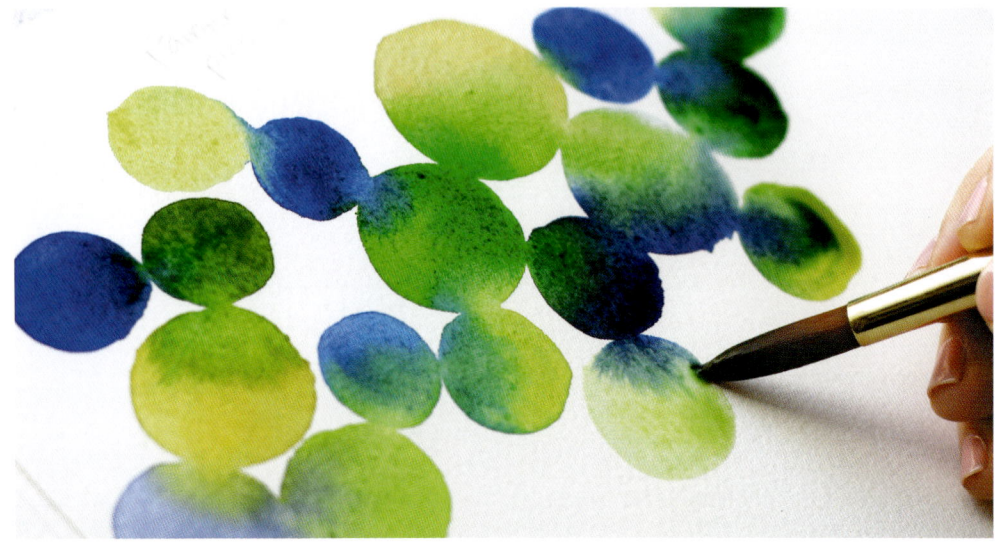

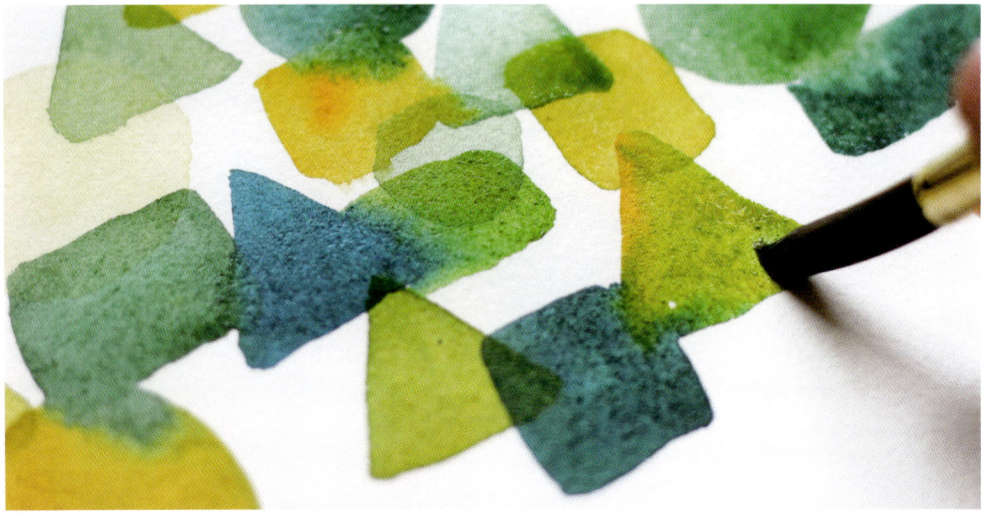

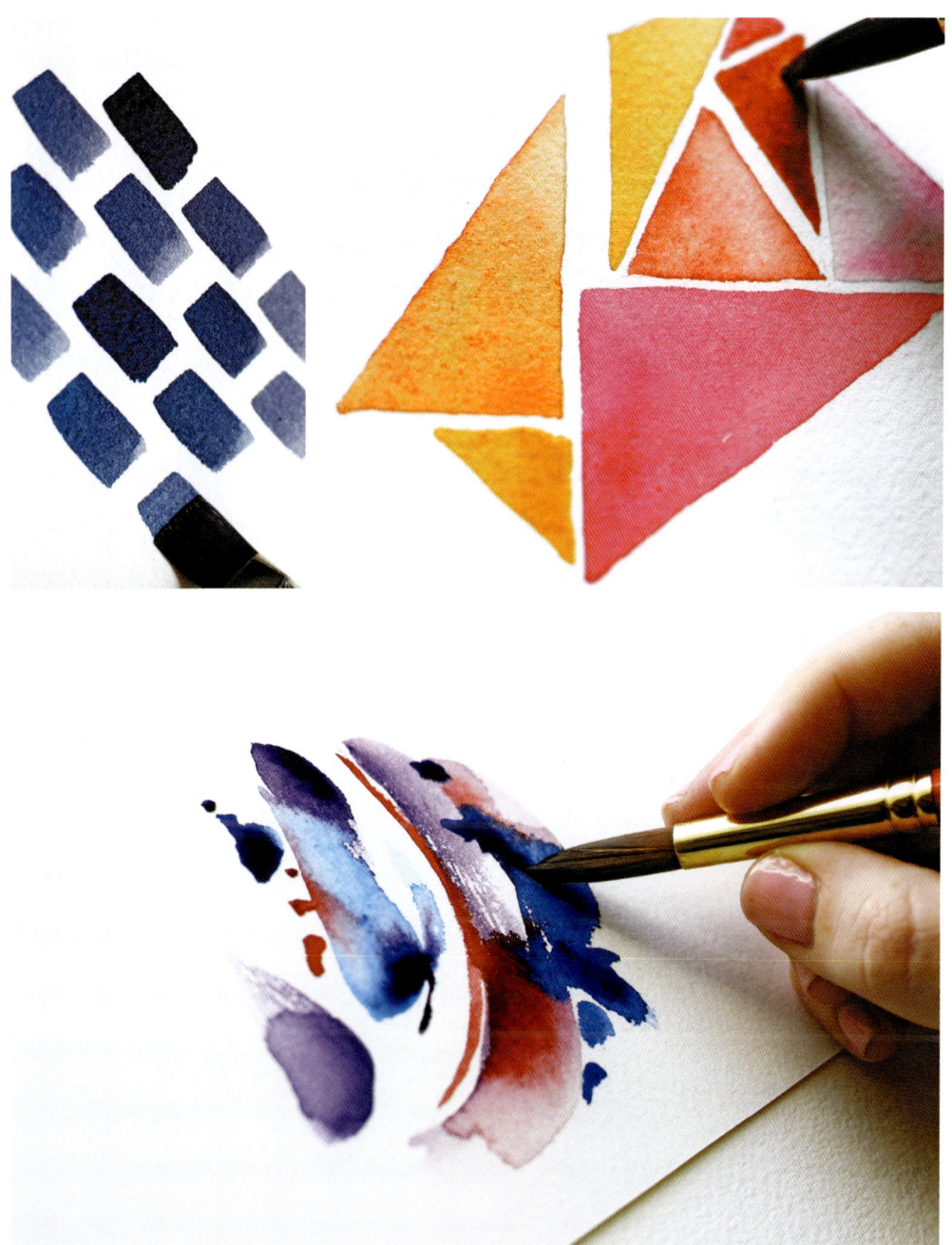

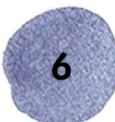

*The basic brushstroke principles also apply to watercolor lettering. You can use the body of the brush, as well as the tip, and will utilize pressure in the brushstrokes. I love creating letters and phrases with watercolor because it gives the lettering character and texture.*

I prefer to use a water brush when creating watercolor letters. This is my favorite tool because it has a super-pointed tip that's perfect for fine lines but can also be pressed down for thicker brushstrokes.

**Downstroke**  **Upstroke**

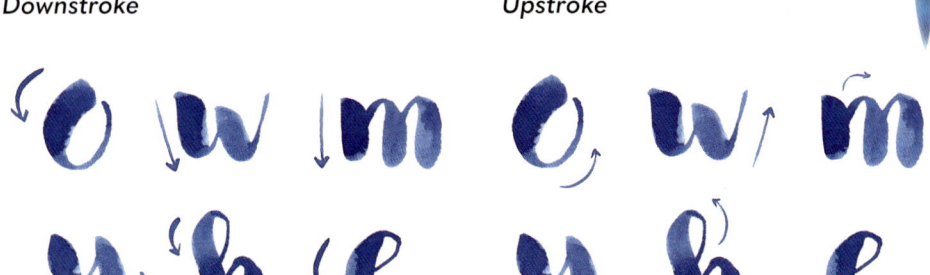

In lettering, there are upstrokes and downstrokes. Downstrokes are thick, and upstrokes are thin. You can use what you've learned about brushstrokes to explore creating downstrokes and upstrokes in the letters.

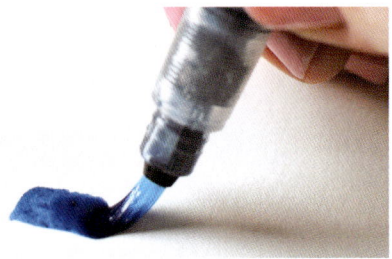

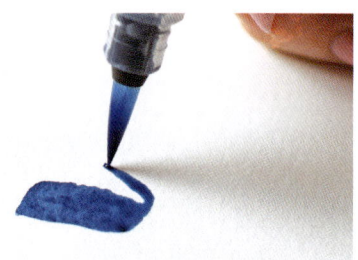

Press down on the full body of the bristles to create thick lines. These are the downstrokes of the letters.

Use the tip of the bristles for thin lines. These are the upstrokes of the letters.

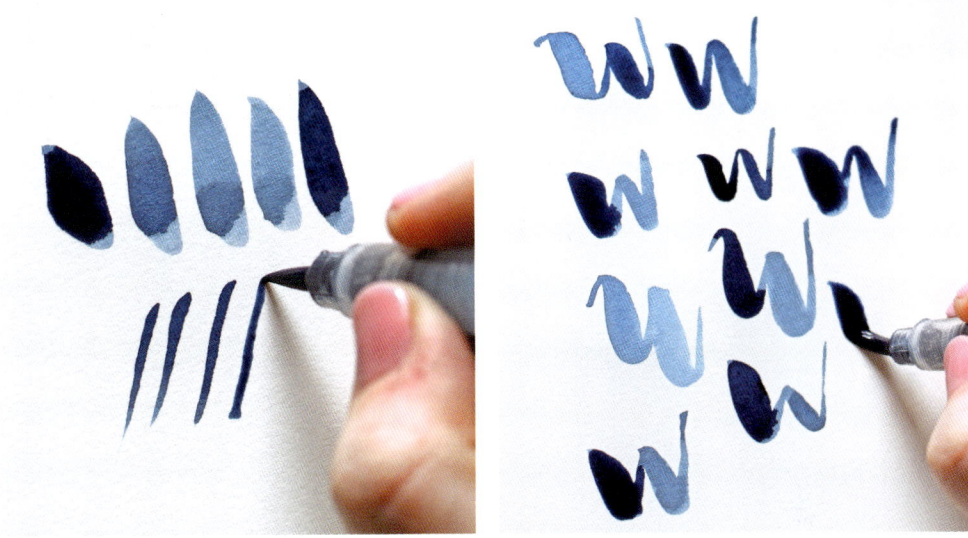

Practice making thick downstrokes with the body of the brush and light upstrokes with the tip. Then, try putting them together by making a continuous, smooth transition from downstroke to upstroke to downstroke again. The letter "W" is perfect for practicing this exercise.

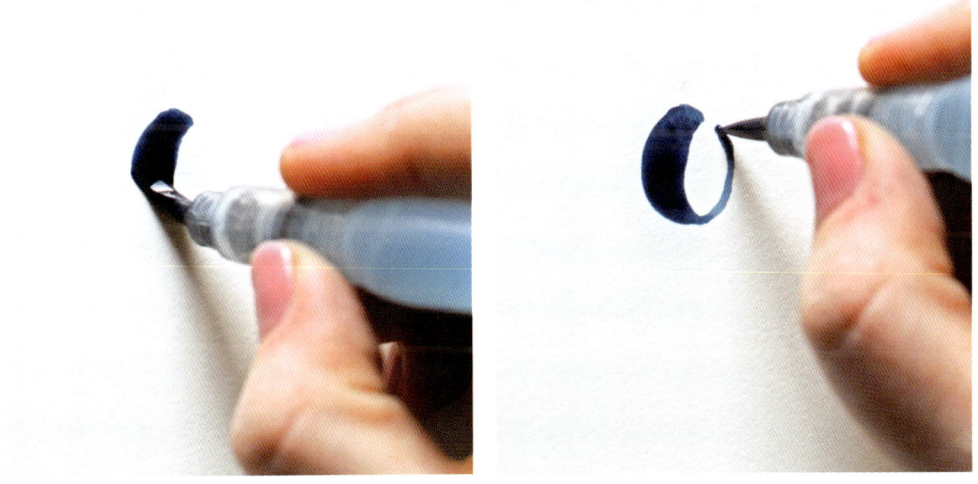

Next, practice curvy letters like "O." As you reach the bottom of the thick downstroke, transition to a thin upstroke on your way back to complete the letter.

*There are many different lettering styles to explore while creating watercolor letters. Paper choice also plays a part in the look of your lettering. Rough, cold-pressed paper yields a very textured look. Smooth, hot-pressed paper yields a smooth, clean look. Both styles are great and work well for a variety of projects.*

**LOVE** *dance*

These are examples of lettering on rough, cold-pressed watercolor paper.

**BLOOM** *thrive*

These are examples of lettering on smooth, hot-pressed watercolor paper.

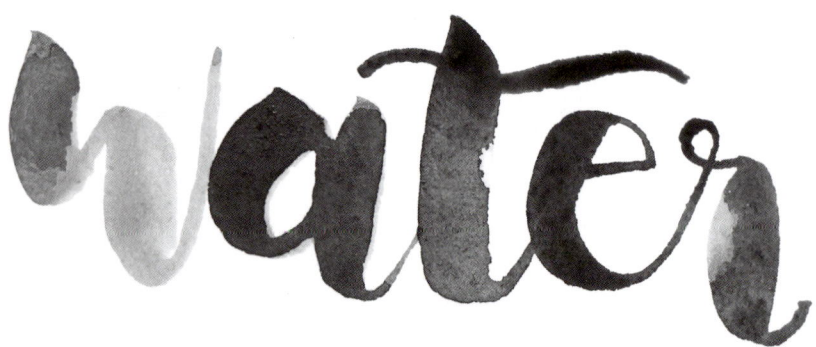

Practice painting the word "water" using a cursive font on smooth, hot-pressed watercolor paper. If you like, you can sketch out the lettering in pencil before painting. Be mindful of whether you are painting an upstroke or downstroke, and adjust your pressure accordingly.

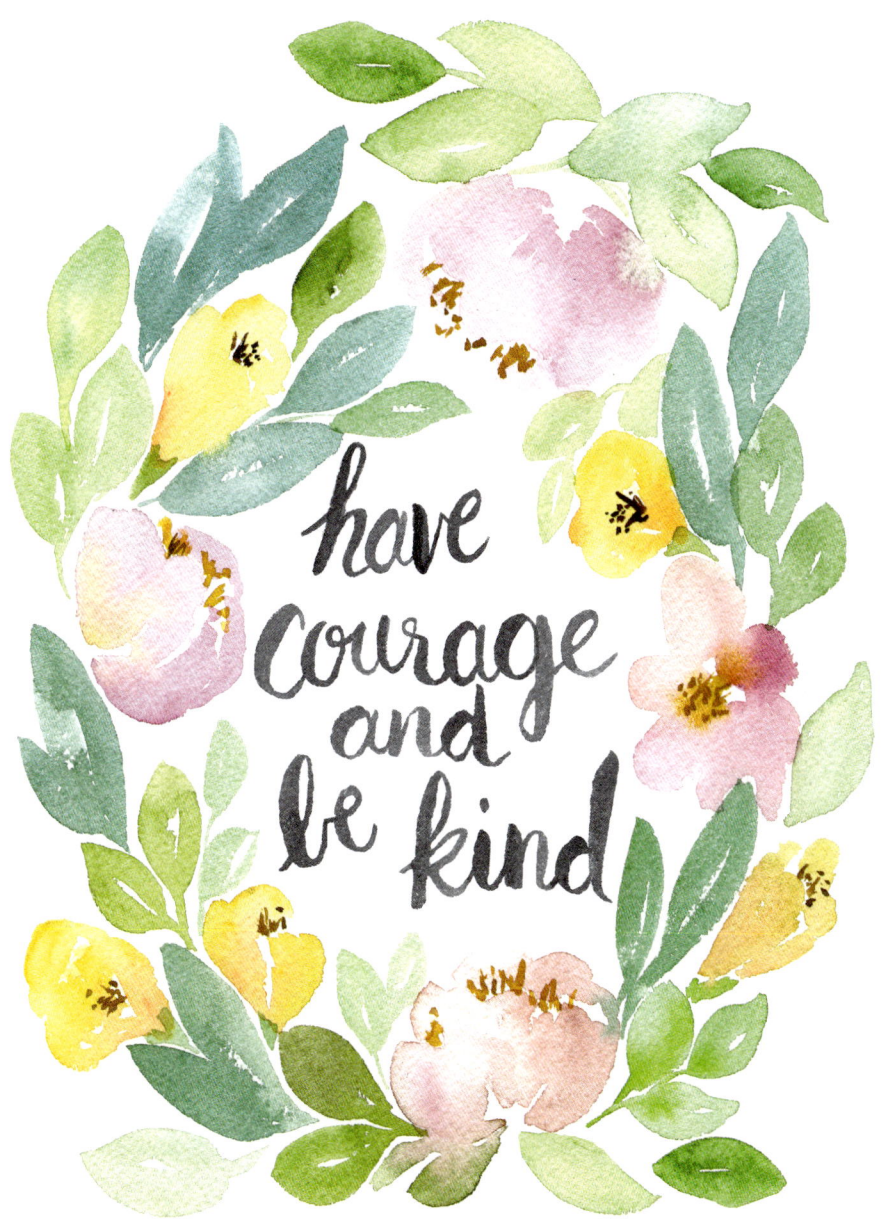

*Masking fluid is one of my favorite materials. It allows you to create unique patterns and keeps the whites of your paper white! Masking fluid is easy to use—experiment with prompts on the next few pages!*

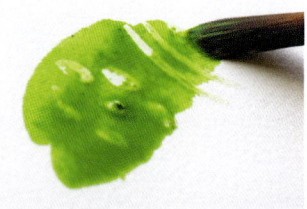

Allow the fluid to dry. Then, apply paint.

Apply masking fluid with a paintbrush. You'll want to use separate paintbrushes for masking fluid and painting, as masking fluid is tough on the bristles.

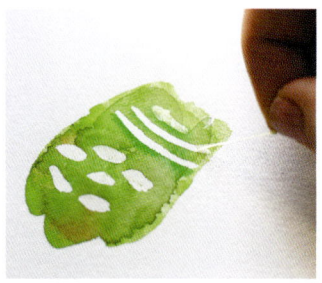

Allow the paint to dry. Then, gently peel the masking fluid off.

## MASKING FLUID TIPS

- Try not to layer on masking fluid too thick. A thin, even layer is perfect. The thicker the layer, the longer it will take to dry.
- Do not paint over masking fluid until it is completely dry.
- Allow paint to dry completely before removing masking fluid.
- Use your finger or an eraser to lightly remove the masking fluid.

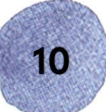

# USE THE WHITE OF THE PAPER

*Masking fluid is a great tool to keep your whites white. Because watercolor is a fluid medium, it's hard to completely control. Use masking fluid to protect pieces of the paper in your work where you don't want any paint.*

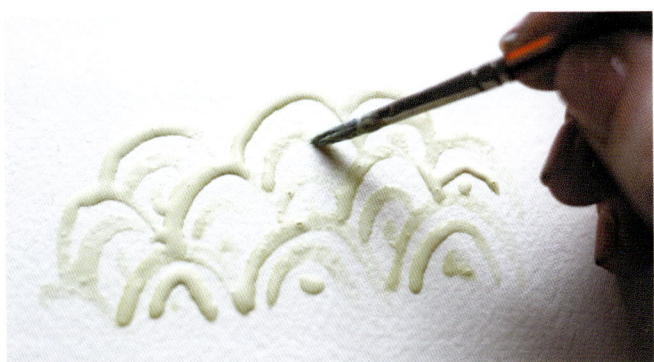

Apply masking fluid just like you would paint. If need be, you can use a pencil to lightly sketch your design first.

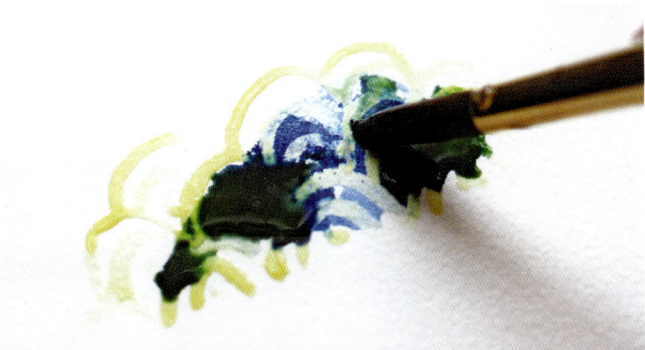

Paint over the masking fluid with the colors of your choice and allow the paint to dry thoroughly.

Peel off the masking fluid gently to reveal the design.

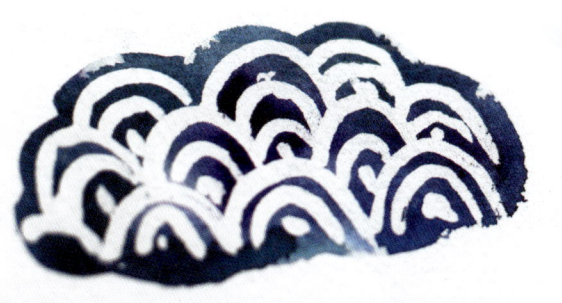

# PROTECT COLORS & CREATE TEXTURE

*You can also use masking fluid to maintain any color that you've already applied.*

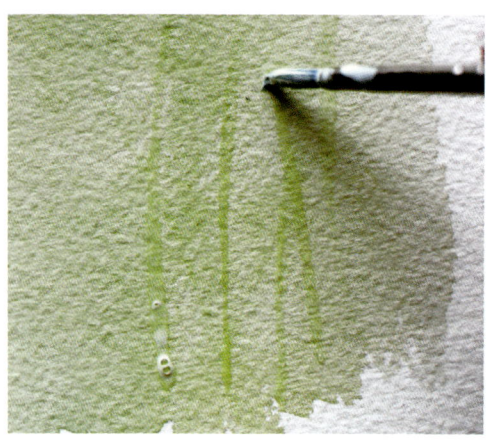

After you have applied paint, allow it to dry before applying masking fluid to the areas you want to protect.

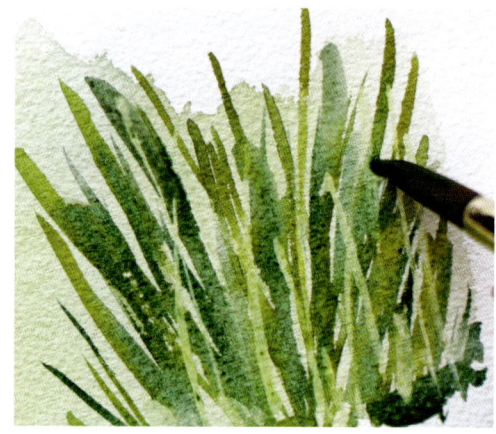

Once the masking fluid is dry, you can apply paint over it.

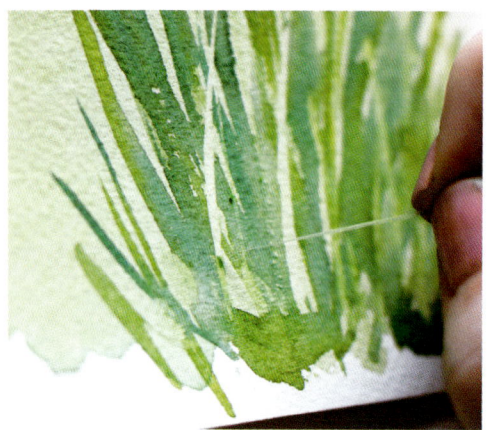

Gently peel off the masking fluid. The original color is preserved!

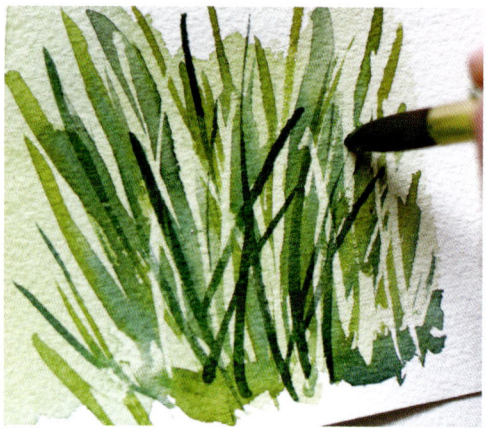

This is a great layering technique to build texture.

**12**

# EXPERIMENT WITH MASKING TAPE

*Artist's masking tape is ideal for creating sharp lines. You can use it to create perfect lines for horizons, geometric shapes, patterns, and more.*

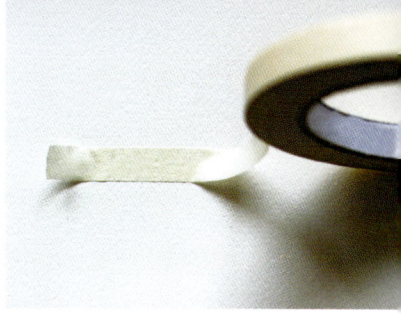

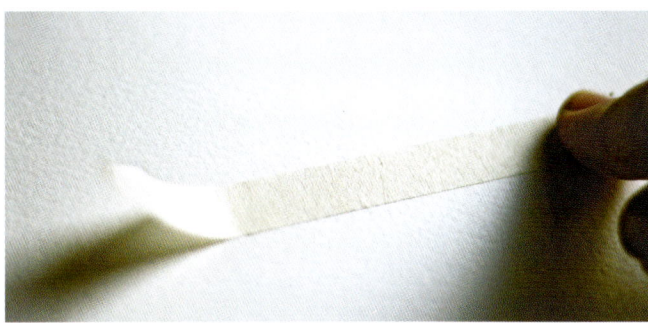

Apply the masking tape. Be sure to press it down tightly to prevent paint from leaking underneath.

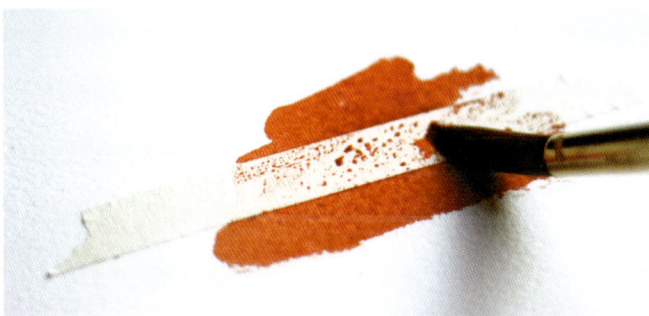

Paint over the tape, and allow the paint to dry thoroughly.

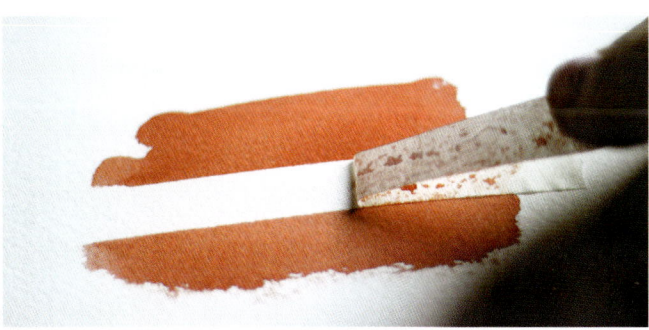

Once the paint is dry, gently peel off the masking tape at an angle to avoid tearing the paper.

# CREATE A NEGATIVE-SPACE PATTERN

*Masking tape is also perfect for painting geometric patterns. Here's just one example. You can follow along, or you can experiment with creating your own patterns.*

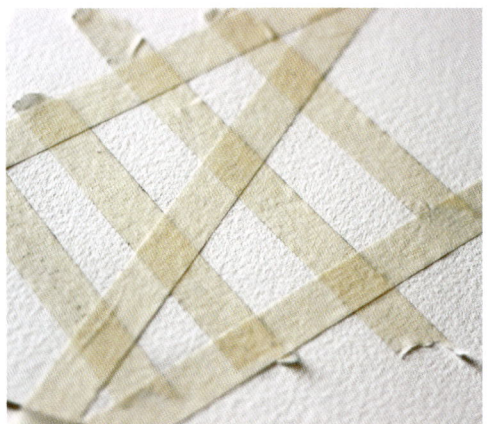

Apply strips of tape to create a pattern. I've created an asymmetrical grid.

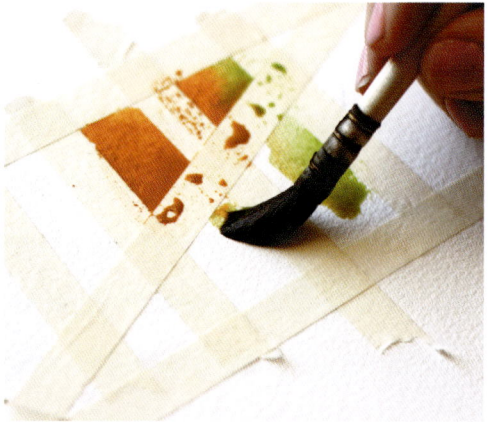

Paint over the pattern with the colors of your choice.

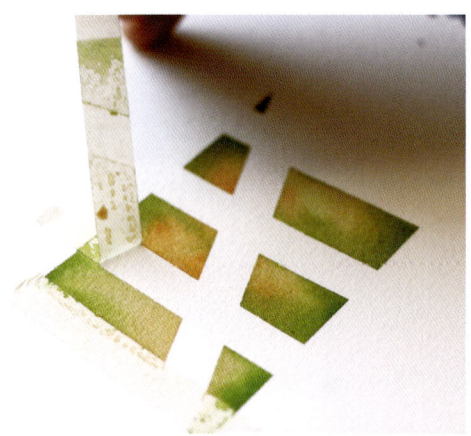

Allow the paint to dry completely before peeling off the tape.

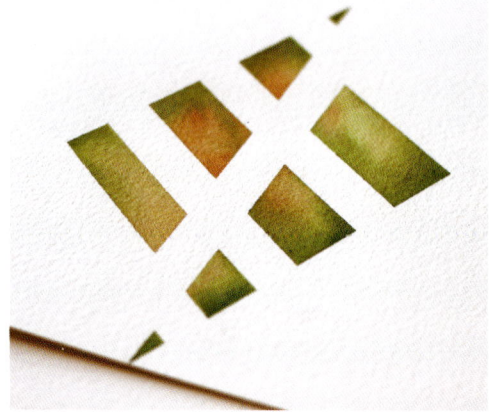

The result is perfect geometric shapes with crisp, even lines.

# PAINT A SUNSET WITH MASKING TAPE

*Here's how you can use the masking tape technique to get a crisp horizon line in a landscape painting.*

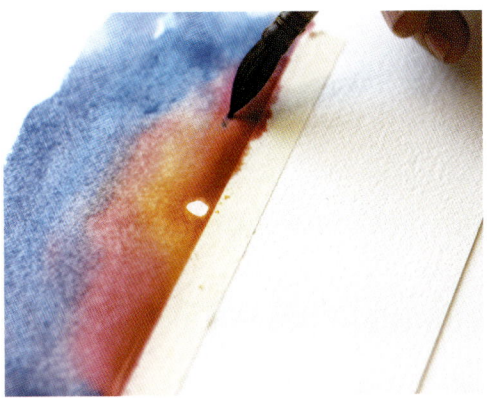

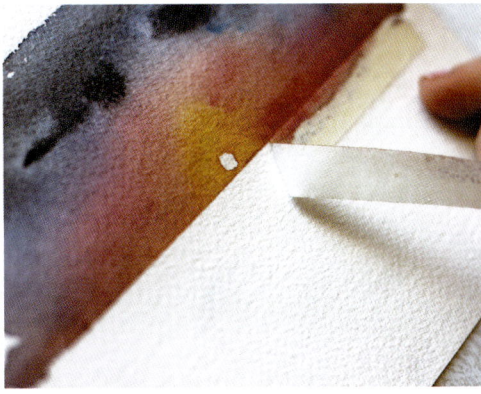

Place a strip of masking tape down where the horizon line is. Then, paint the sky or background above the tape, bringing the paint all the way down to the tape.

Let the paint dry before gently peeling off the masking tape.

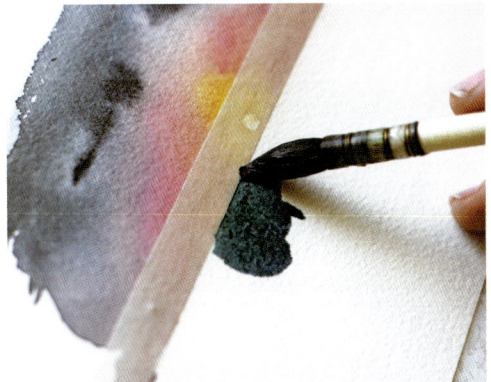

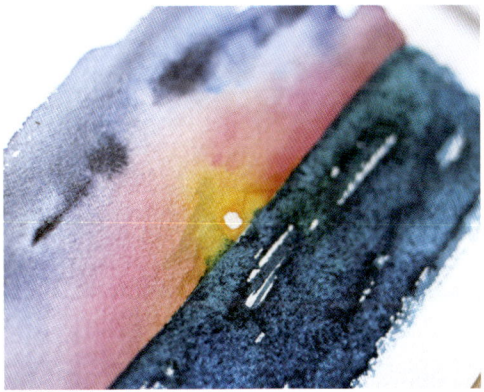

Reapply a new piece of masking tape, aligning the bottom edge of the tape strip with the horizon line. Then, paint the bottom half of the scene.

When the paint is dry, gently peel away the masking tape to reveal your beautiful landscape!

# 15 CREATE A RESIST WITH ALCOHOL

*You can use alcohol to create unique textures in watercolor. Alcohol pushes the paint away, creating white shapes. You can use regular rubbing alcohol for this technique. It works best when the paint is still a bit wet.*

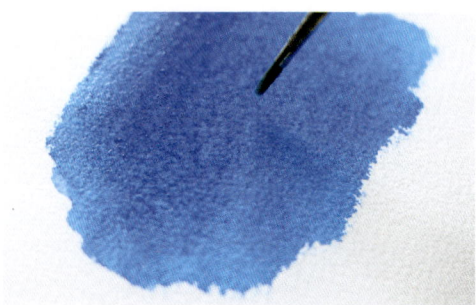

First, apply paint to the watercolor paper.

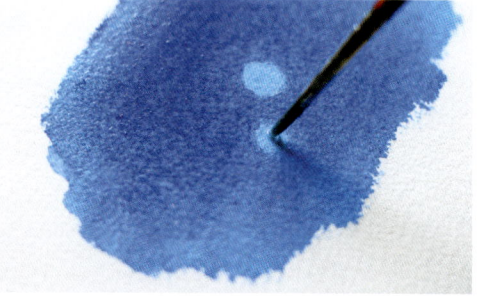

Use a paintbrush to apply alcohol to the paint while it is still wet.

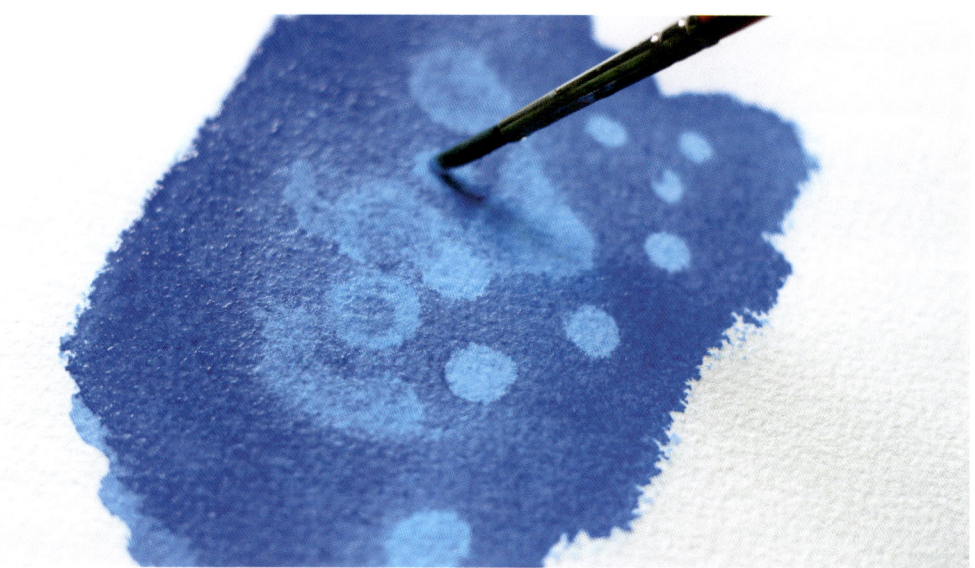

The result is subtler than masking fluid or tape, producing soft, feathery markings.

## 16 CREATE A RESIST WITH SALT

*Another way to create resist texture is to use salt on a wet wash. The salt gathers some of the pigment, creating a starry effect.*

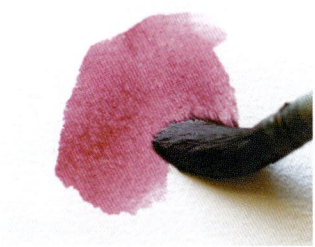 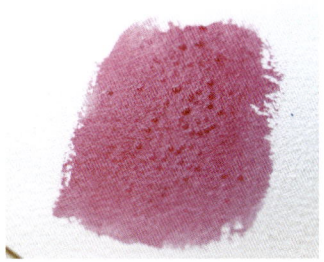 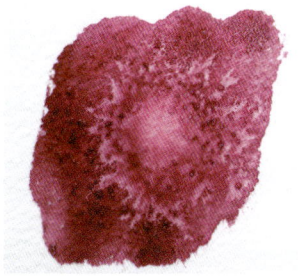

Start by laying down a watercolor wash.

Allow the paint to dry slightly, and then sprinkle salt over the still-wet wash.

Allow the paint to dry, and then brush off the salt. The size of the salt grains and the wetness of the paper will affect the look.

## 17 COLOR WITH CRAYON FIRST

*You can also use a white crayon to create a wax resist technique. Water and wax don't mix. When you draw with the crayon on paper first, the paint will bead up on the wax.*

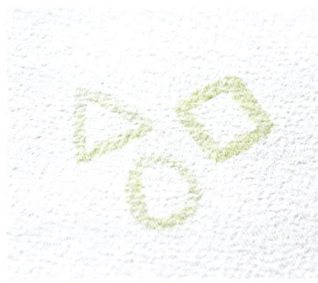 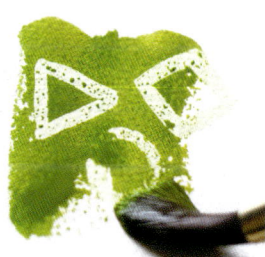 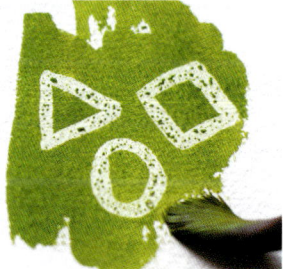

Draw on watercolor paper with a white crayon. I've just drawn some simple shapes.

Apply paint over the wax.

As you paint, you'll see that the shapes or designs you drew in crayon remain free of paint.

# PAINT WITH BLEACH

*While you can't "erase" watercolor paint, it is possible to lift some of the paint off the paper. One way to achieve this is by using bleach. Be sure to use synthetic paintbrushes when working with bleach. Bleach is caustic and will ruin natural hair brushes.*

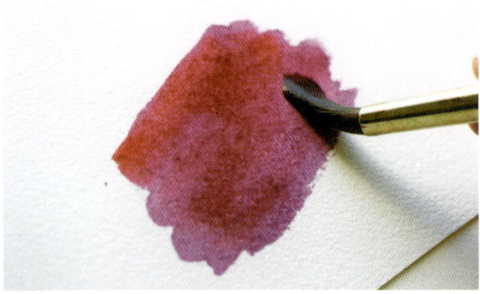

First, apply paint to the watercolor paper.

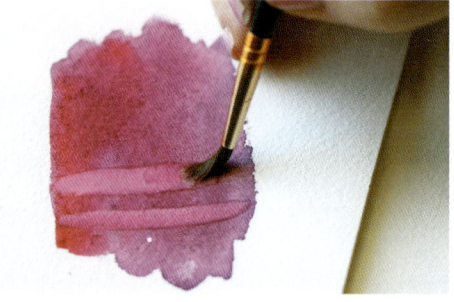

Use a paintbrush to apply alcohol to the paint while it is still wet.

**You can also dilute bleach with water for a subtler look.**

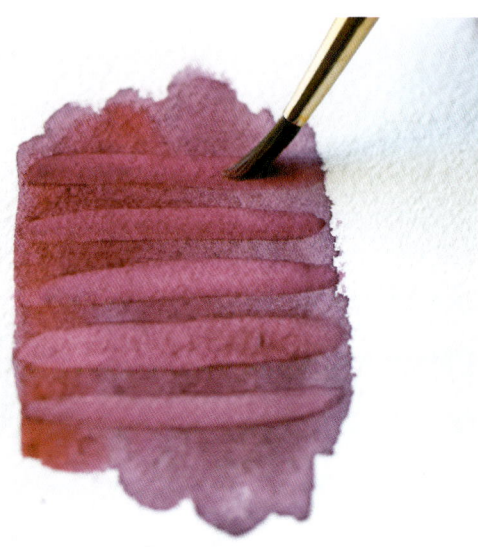

The result is subtler than masking fluid or tape, producing soft, feathery markings.

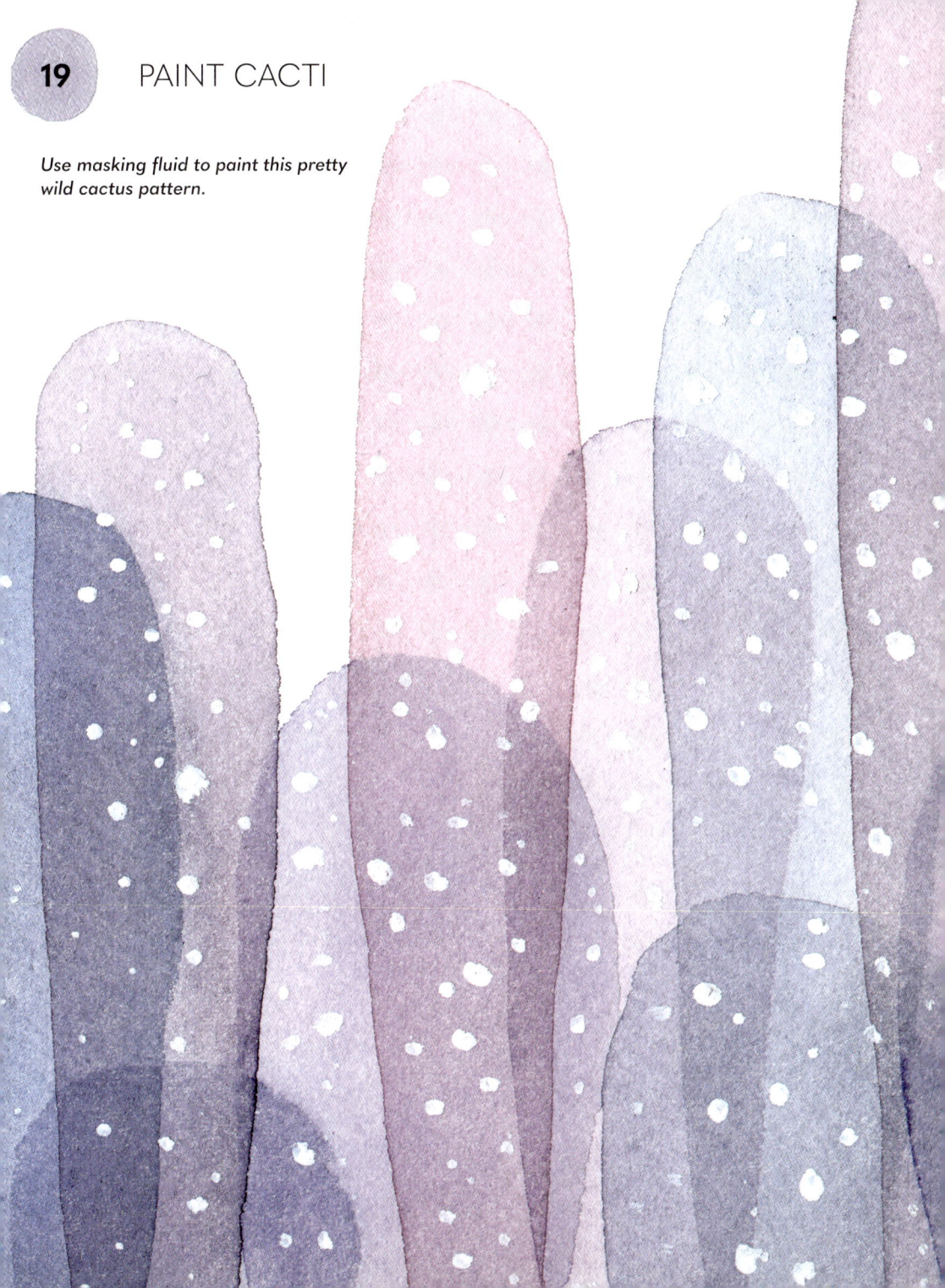

**19** PAINT CACTI

*Use masking fluid to paint this pretty wild cactus pattern.*

*Flowers come in all shapes, sizes, colors, and textures. Some may seem easier to paint than others, but with the tips in this series of prompts, I'll show you how to paint all kinds of flowers—with a little bit of practice, you'll be able to paint all your favorite florals.*

Shown here is an example of a variety of petal shapes. Note how they vary in both shape and size. Petals can be pointed, round, square, jagged, etc. Use the body of the brush for the round edges and the tip of the brush for the pointed edges.

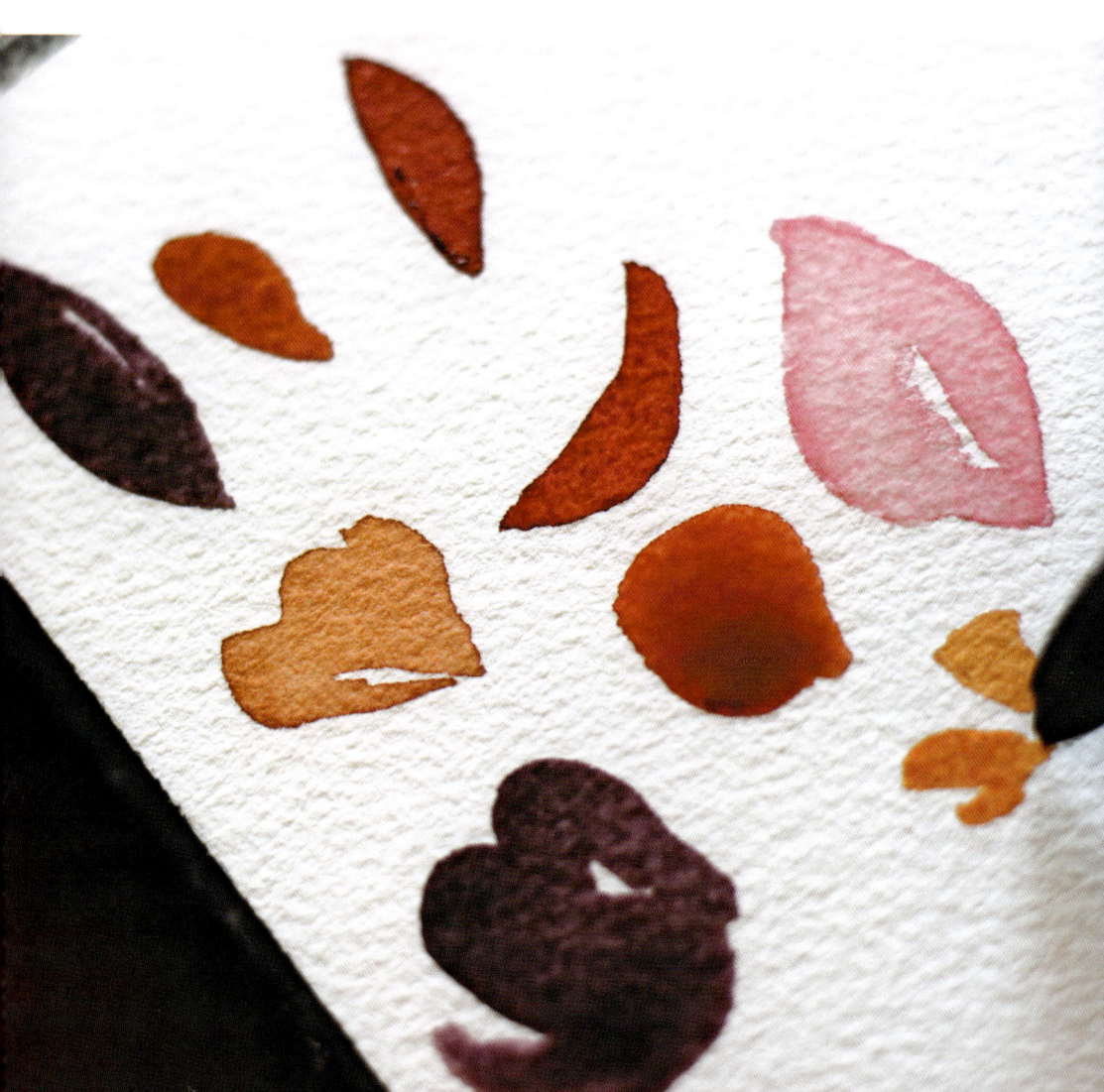

# PAINT BASIC PETAL SHAPES & FLOWER CONES

*Flower petals come together at the stem. As you paint them, think of a cone with the petals fanning out from the center and coming back. The images on this page demonstrate how to think of a flower as a cone. Practice this exercise a few times to warm up!*

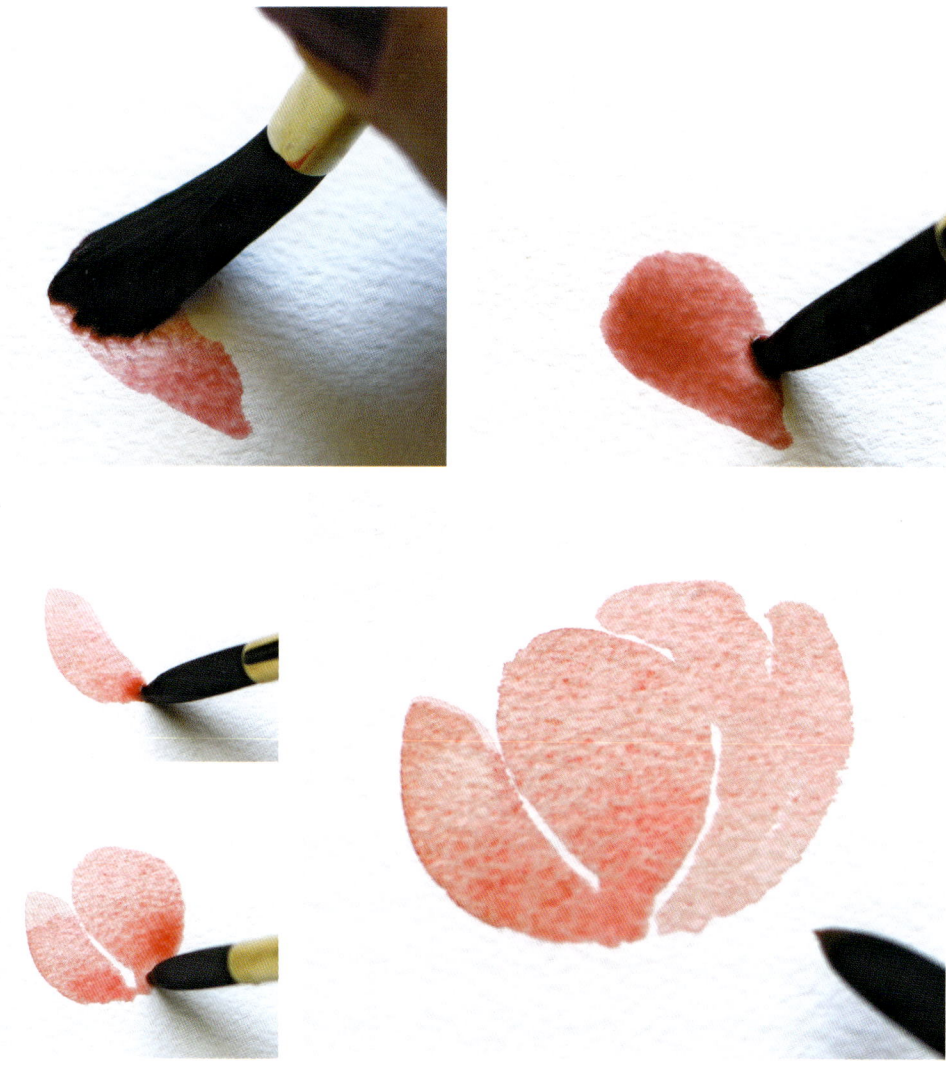

## 22    PLAY WITH VALUE & COLOR IN PETALS

*Add interest and contrast to a flower by adding the same pigment in a darker value or by adding a different pigment.*

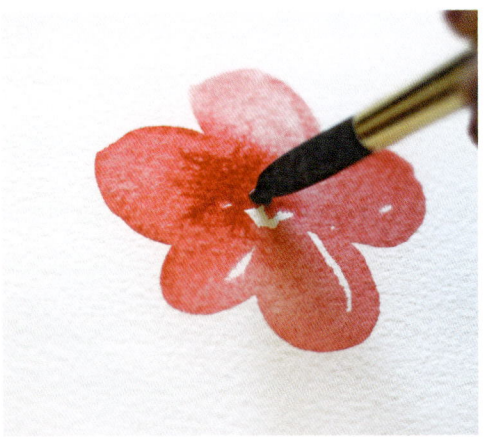
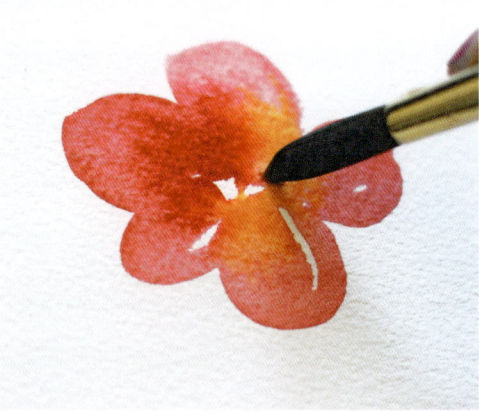

## 23    START AT THE CENTER

*For some flowers, such as sunflowers, you will paint the center first and then create the petals around the middle.*

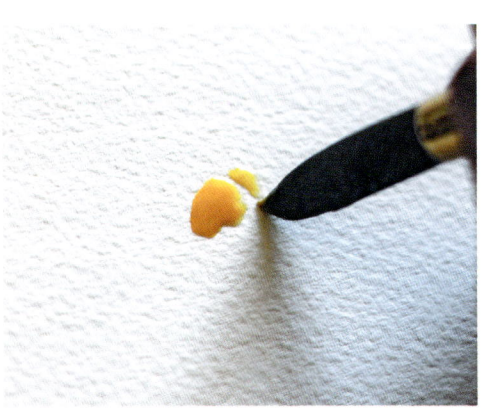
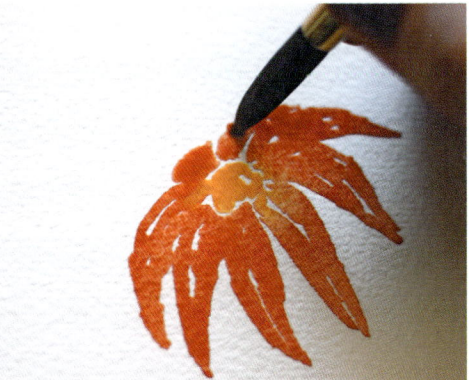

# WORK FROM THE OUTSIDE IN

*For other flowers, such as peonies, you'll paint the flower first and then add the center detail, either wet-on-wet or wet-on-dry.*

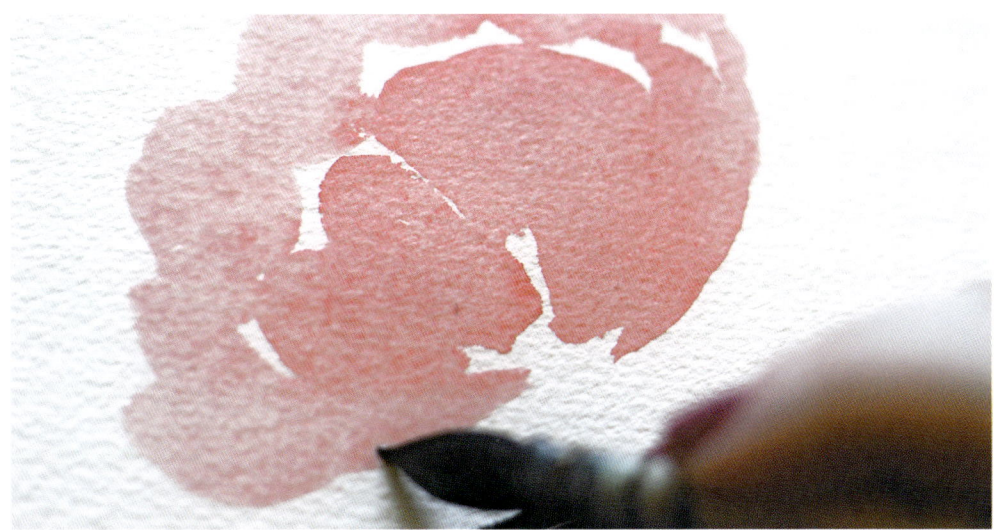

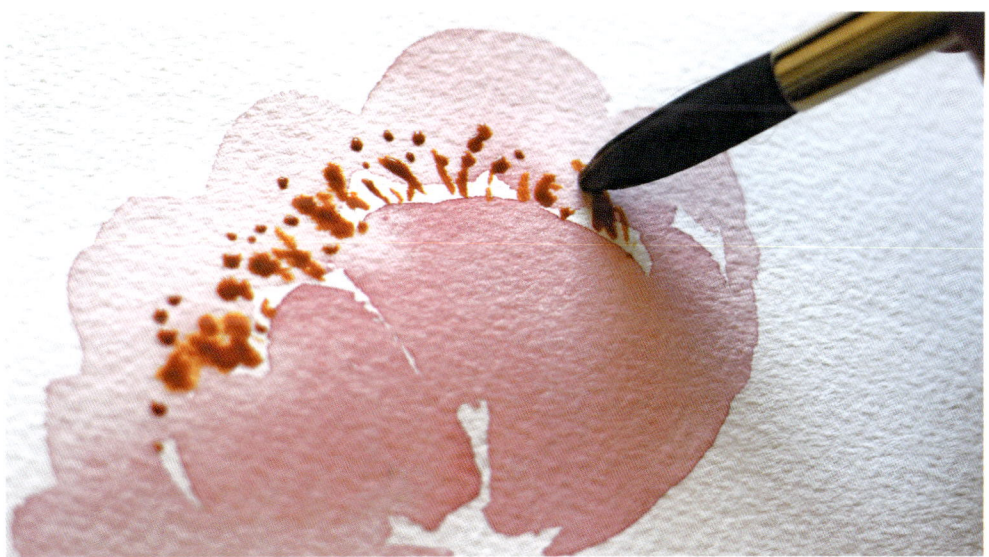

# 25 PAINT PEONIES

*Remember that a flower is like a cone, and all petals point toward the center. Use the body of the paintbrush to make the curvy tops of the petals and the tip of the brush to bring the petals to a point. Use light and dark values to create variety and depth, and add upper layers of petals with a lighter wash. You can create bleeding by adding the yellow center while the pink paint is still wet for a unique look, or you can allow the petals to dry before adding the center.*

*Follow these steps to paint a perfect peony!*

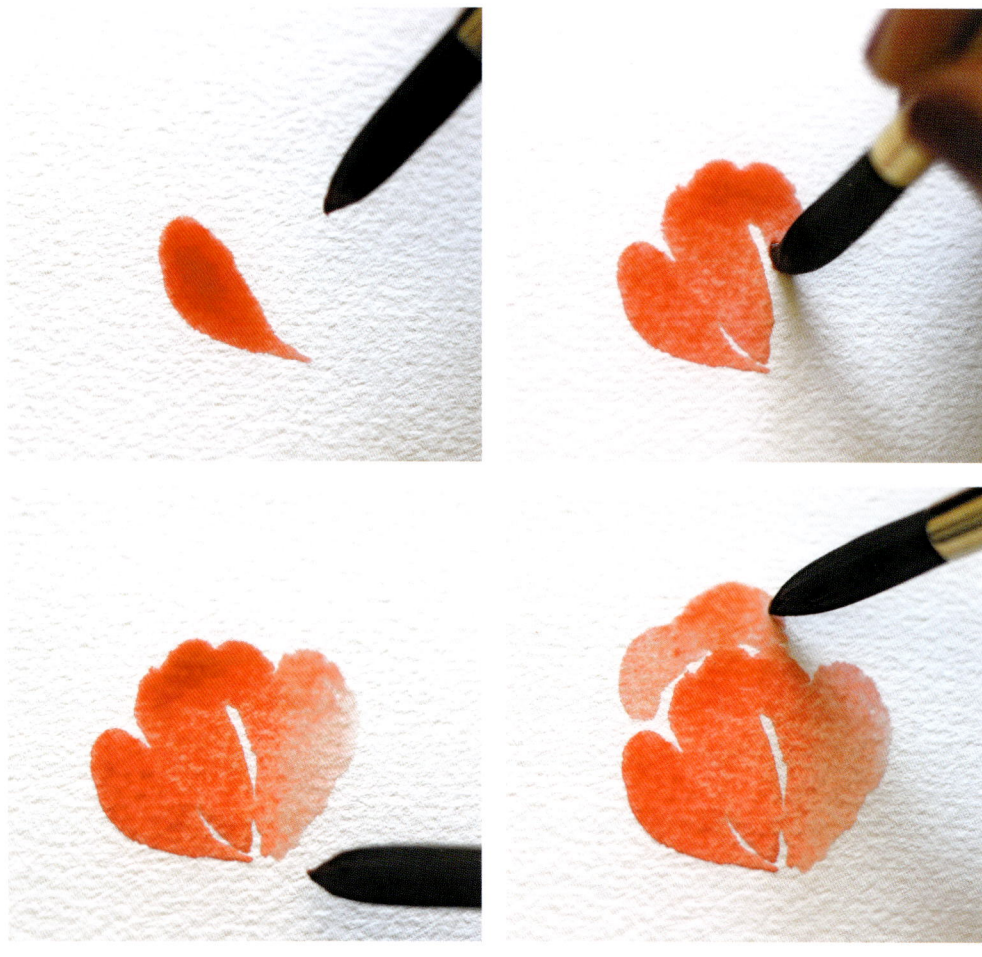

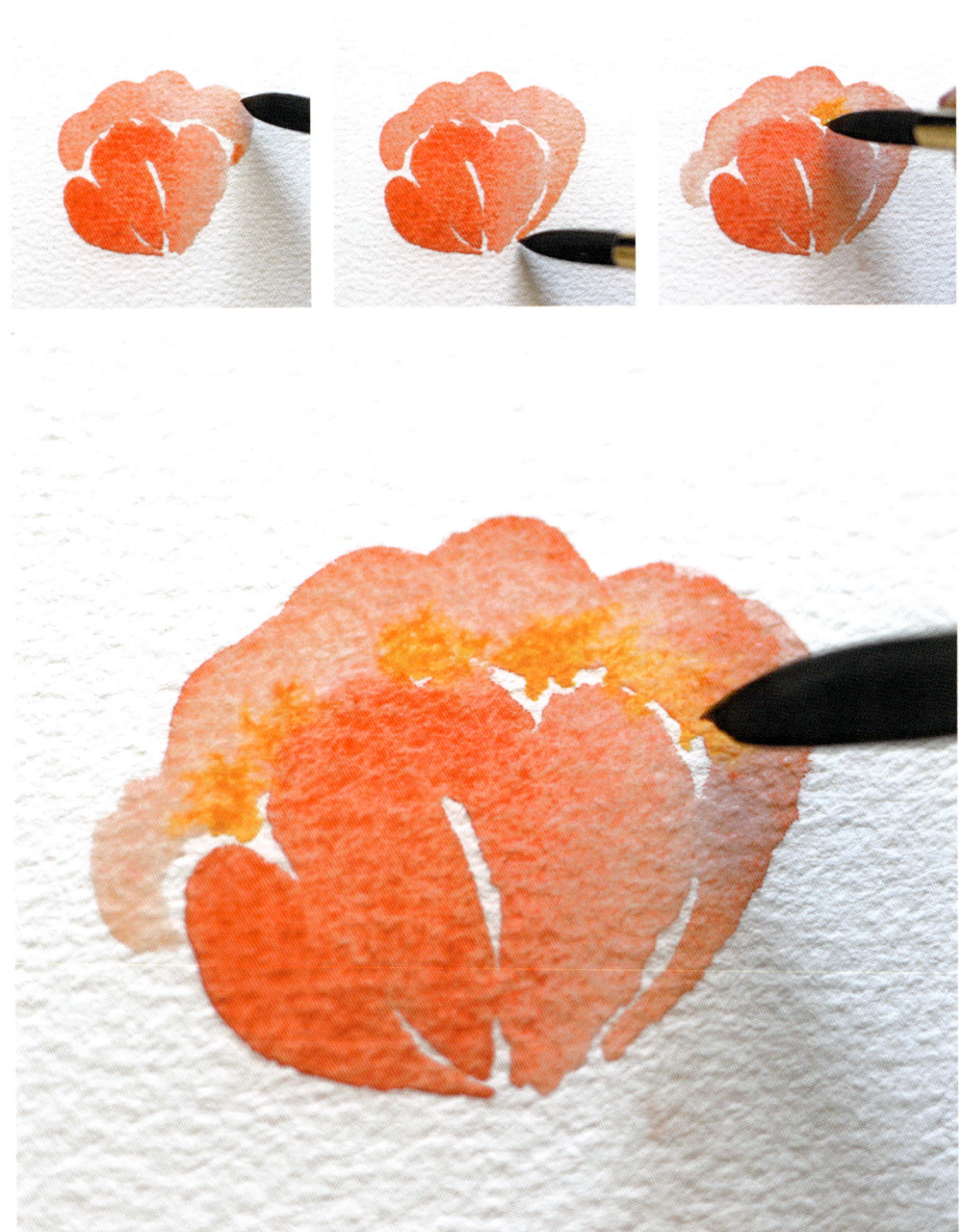

# PAINT ROSES

*When painting a rose, start with a small center circle and three lines around it. Create curved shapes that are more voluminous on one side. Coordinate the petals so that the layers adjacent to one another don't match up. Continue adding layers until the flower is the size you want.*

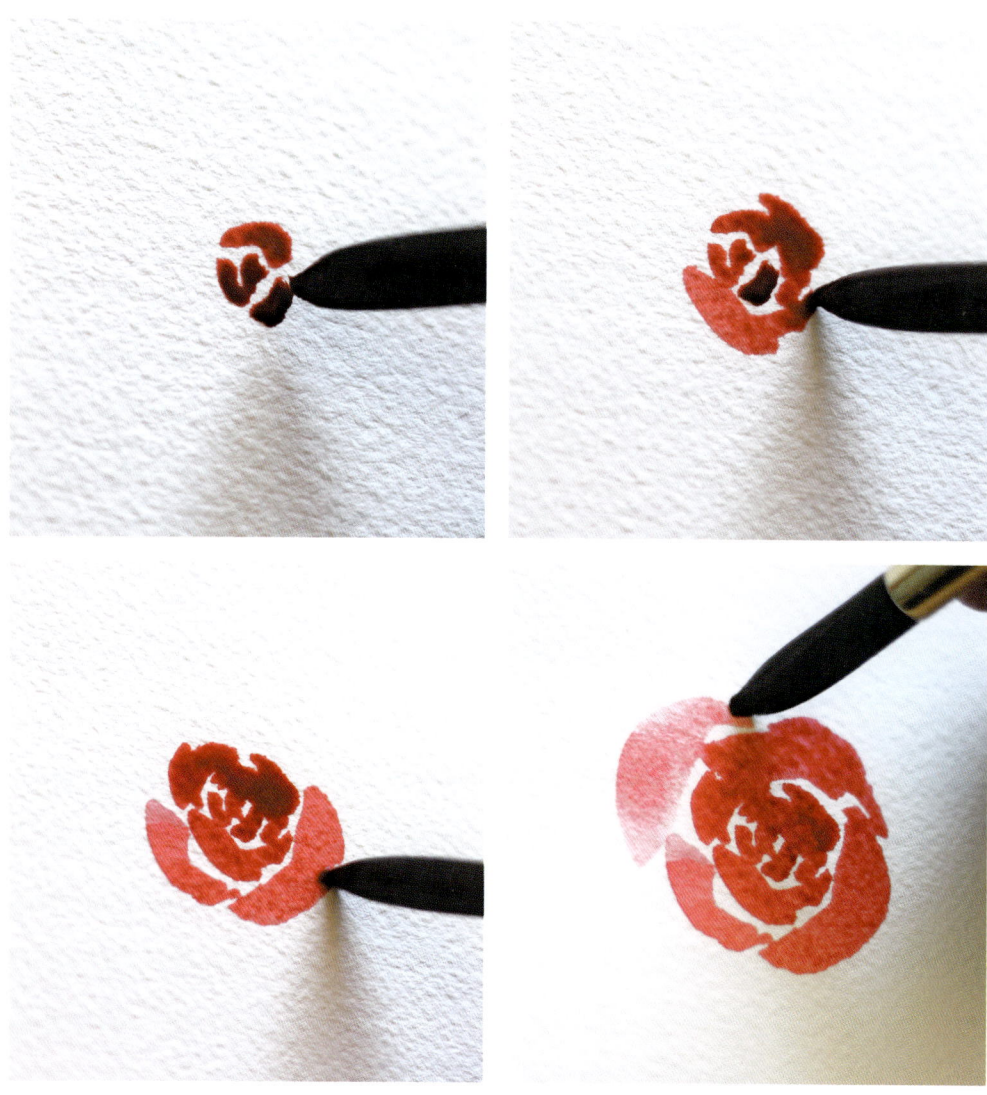

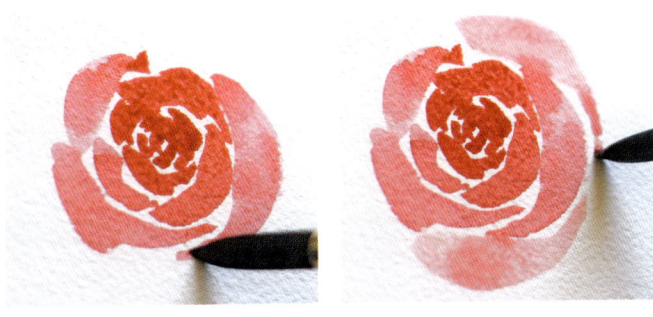

As you move out
from the center,
use less pigment
and more water
to create depth.

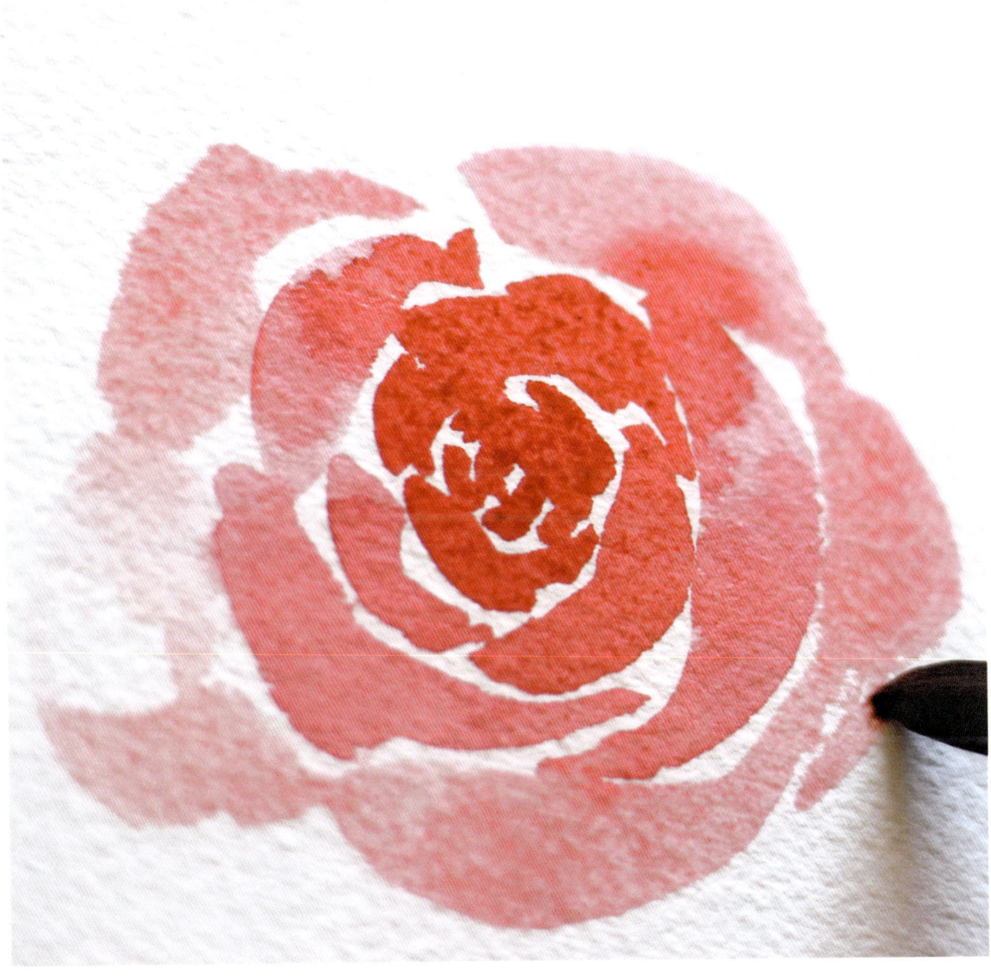

# 27 PAINT OPEN FLOWERS

*For open flowers, such as cosmos and pansies, paint one petal at a time until you reach the desired shape. Mix up the sizes of the petals for a lifelike look, and leave some white space in between for definition and to create the illusion of separation. Add more pigment to create interest and diversity in the petal color.*

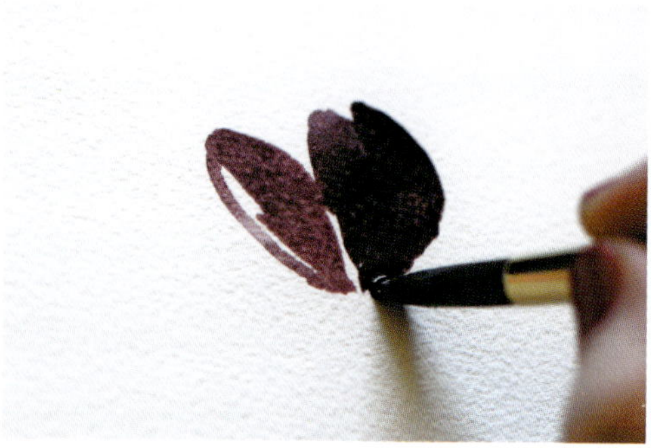

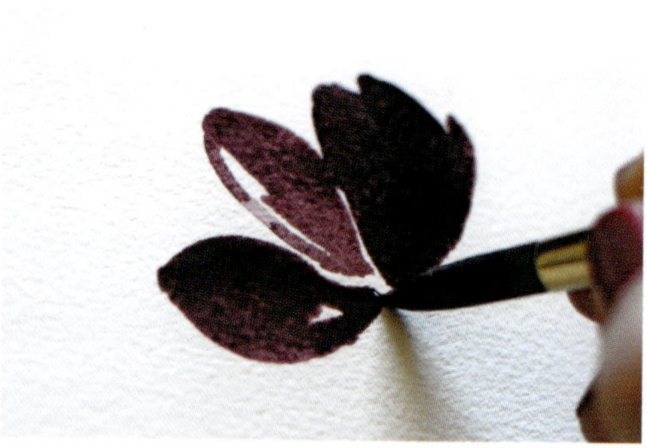

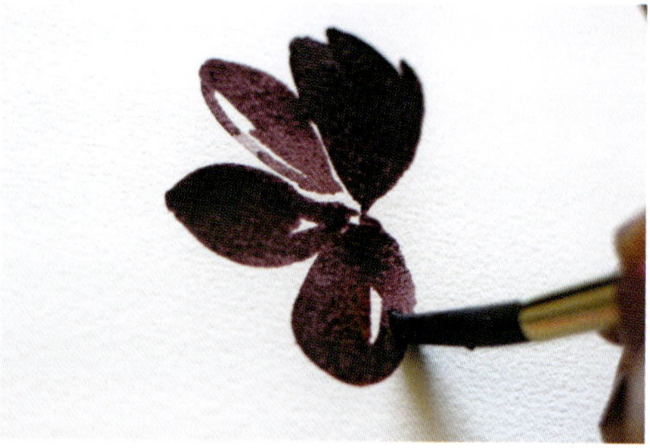

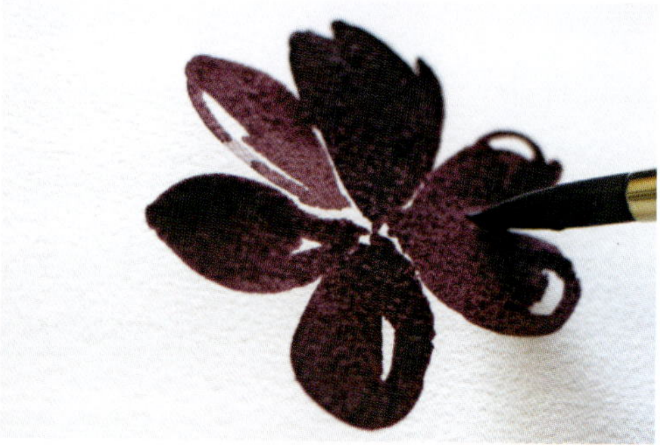

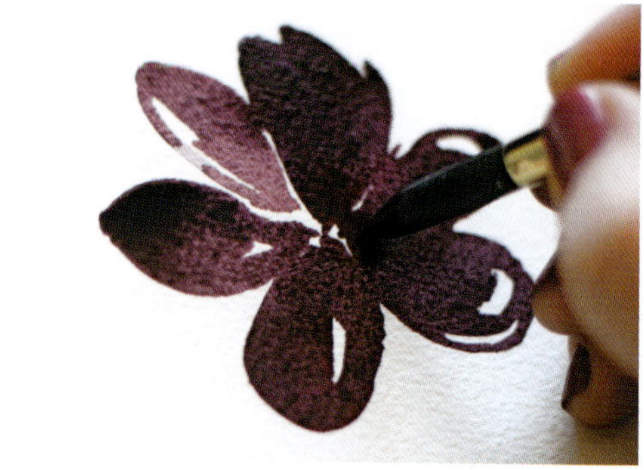

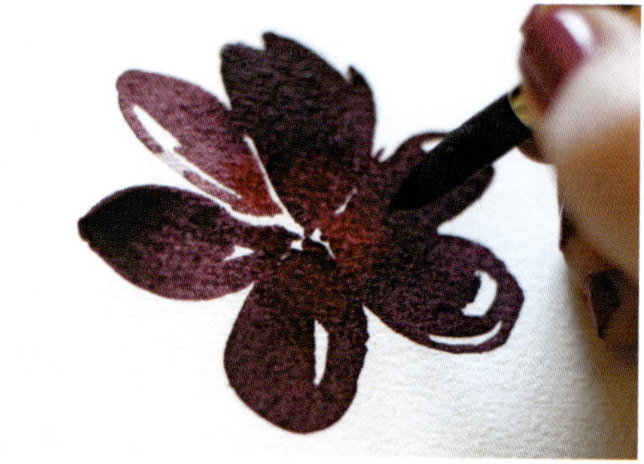

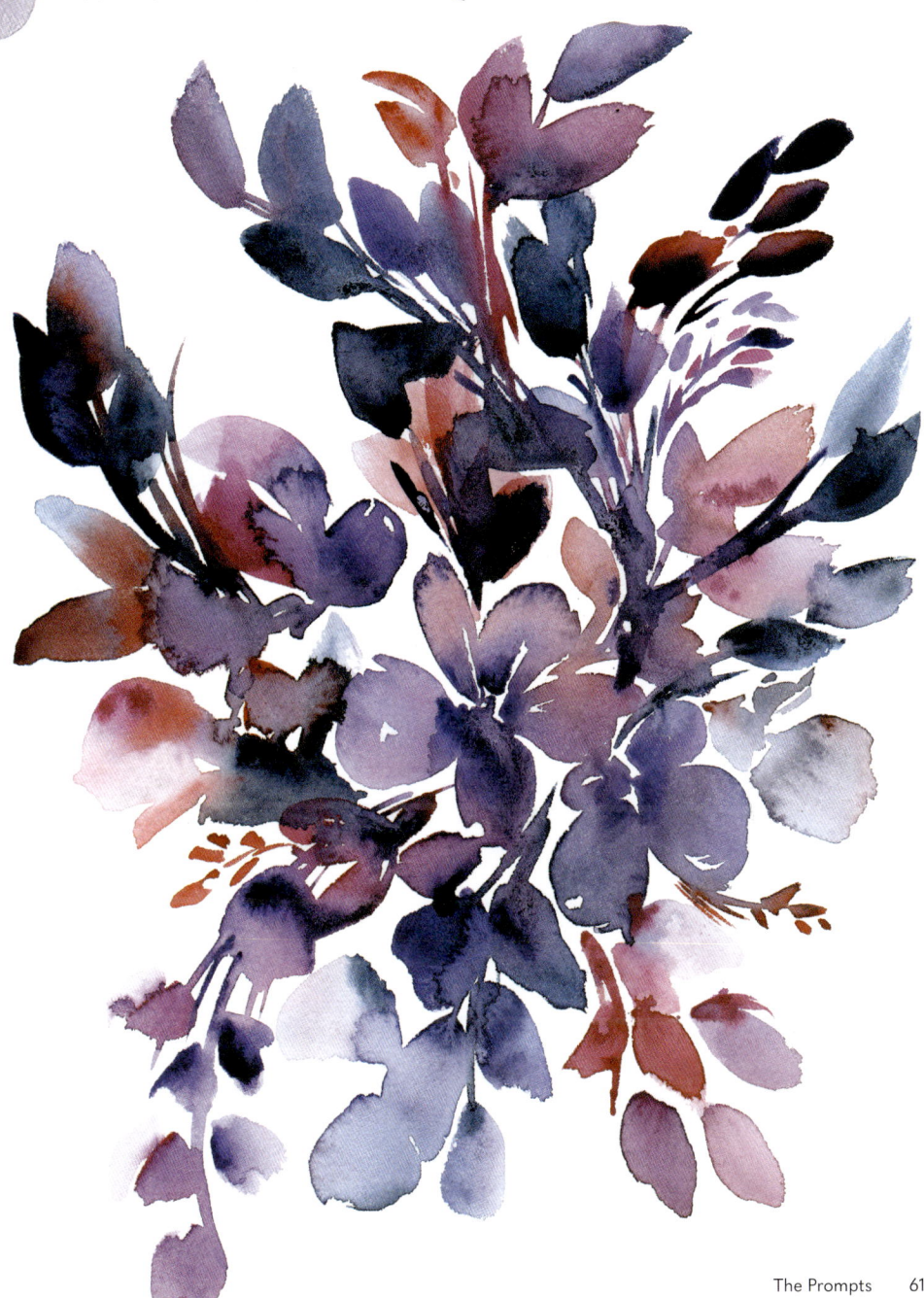

# PAINT CLOSED FLOWERS

Some flowers, such as tulips, are more naturally closed, and the centers are not visible from the side. Paint the petals straight up and slightly curved inward. Create separation of petals with white space or lighter and darker paint values.

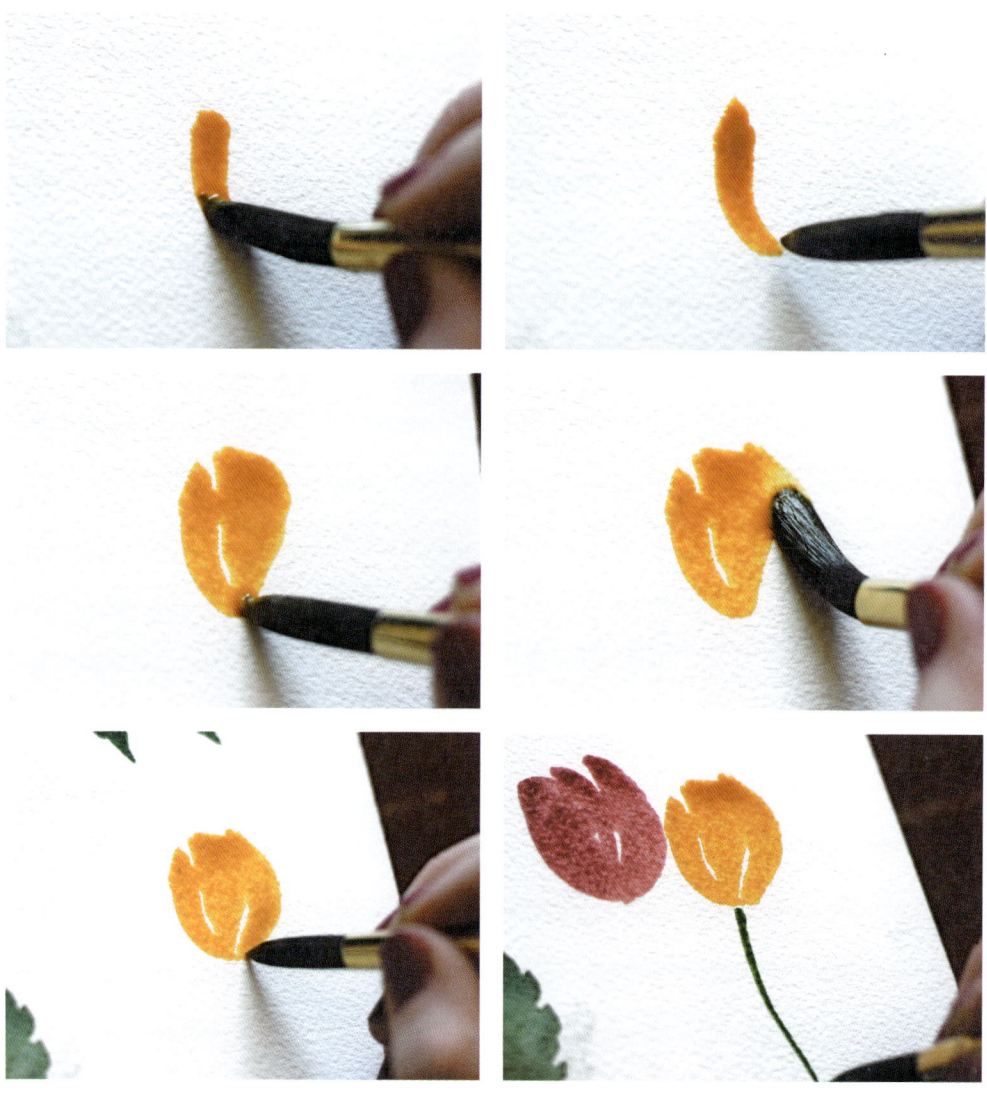

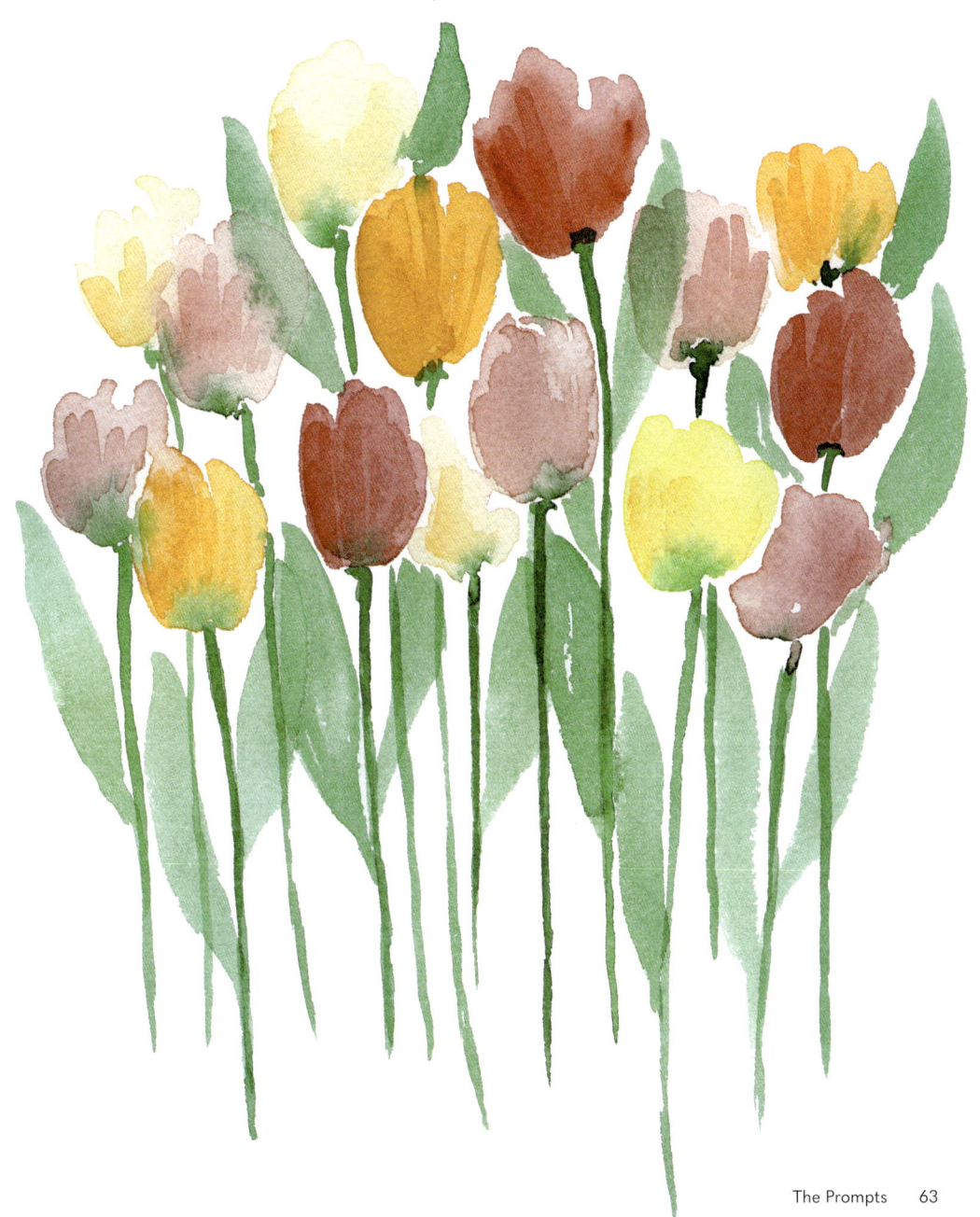

# PAINT SMALL FLOWERS

Some flowers are very small, and there is no need for petal definition or centers. Adding greenery helps define small flowers as a bunch. This is a good technique for painting flowers like hydrangeas or lilacs.

Smaller flowers are usually found in bunches. Create interest by adding flowers that overlap and layer.

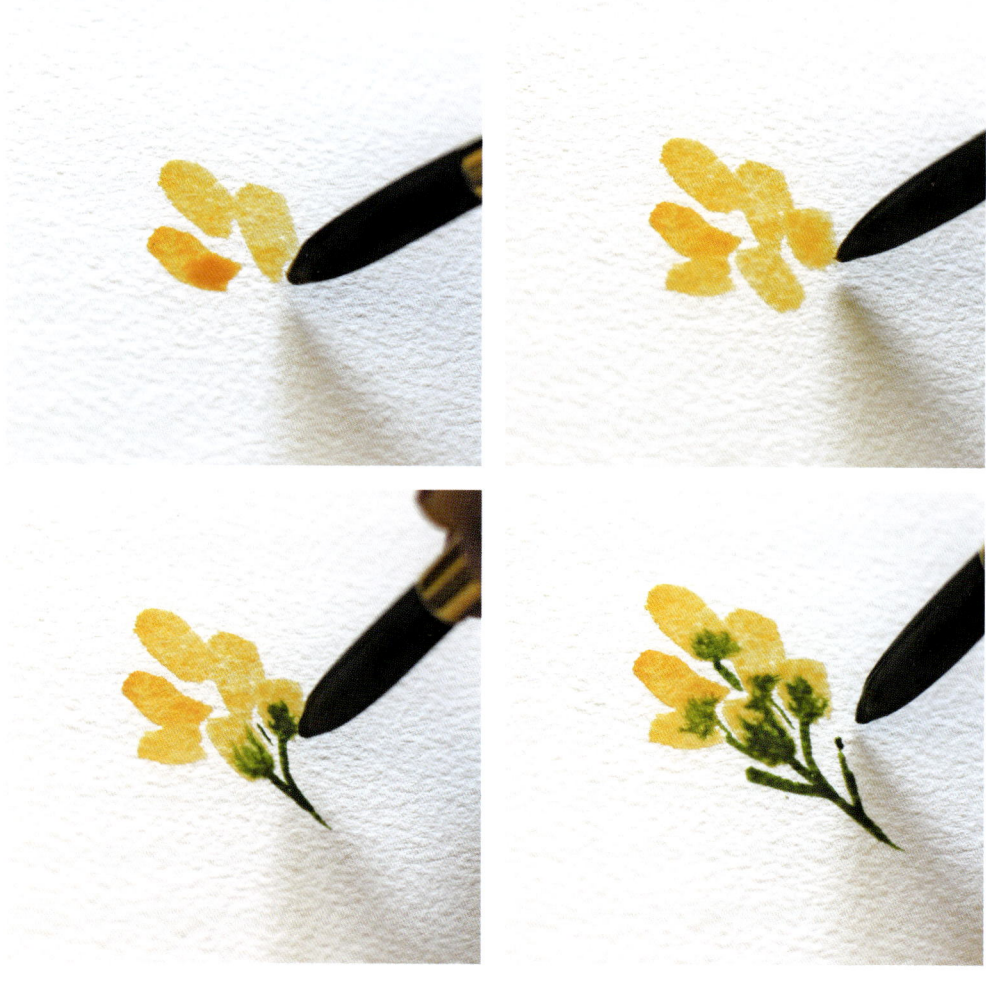

# LET THE COLORS MINGLE

*Letting the green paint bleed into the flower is a fun technique I often use to create variety and interest. Don't be afraid to let the colors mingle and bleed into each other!*

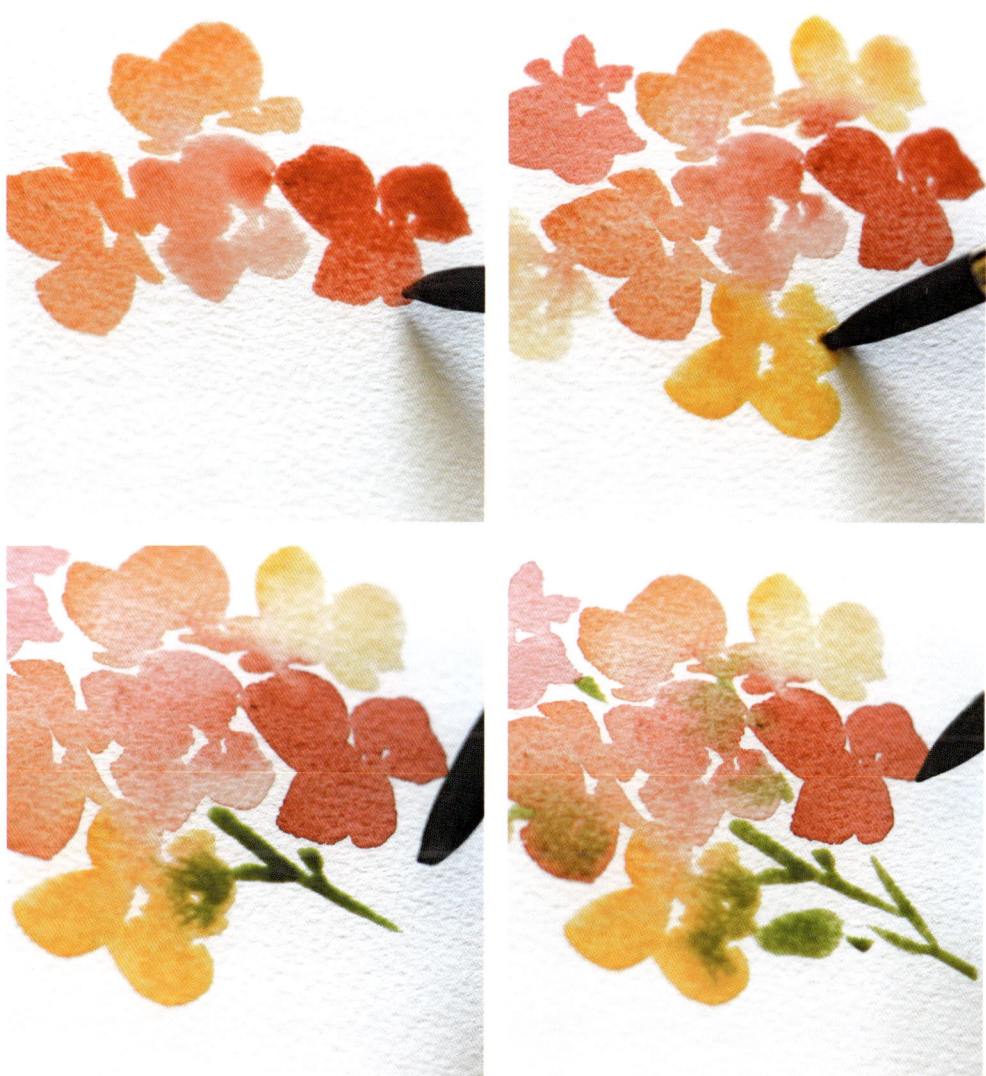

# 33  PAINT A BLACK-AND-WHITE BOUQUET

*Painting in black and white not only helps you practice and learn how to understand color values, but it also creates a pretty, monochrome aesthetic.*

*To understand gray scale and value better, let's compare a picture in full color and black and white. Converting a picture to black and white allows you to better see the light, medium, and dark values.*

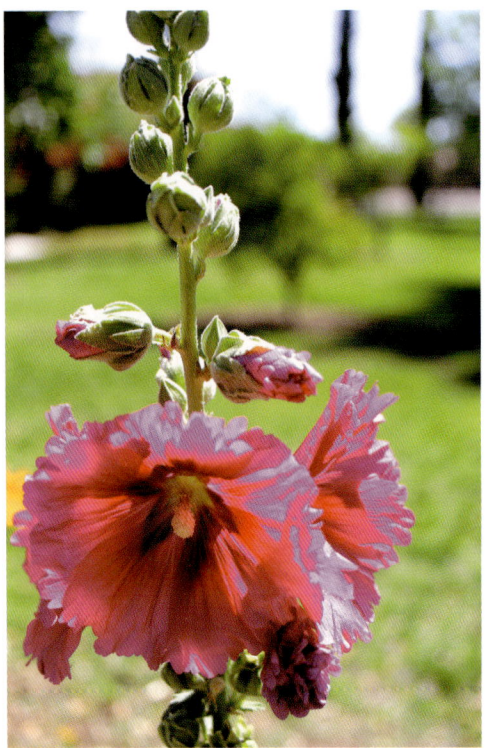
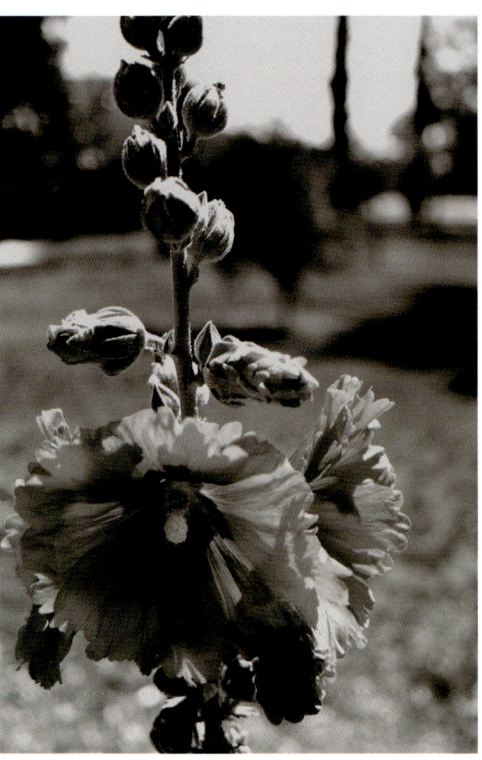

In this example, I show how layering different shades of gray helps me see the color values in the picture. I know where both the darker shades and the bright, almost-white shades are. This is so helpful before painting this piece in color because I can better visualize where the dark color values are.

Paint your own black-and-white bouquet.

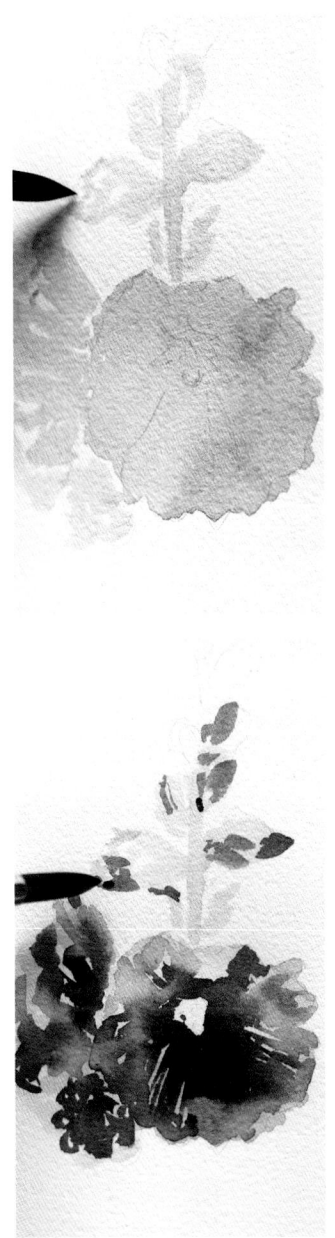

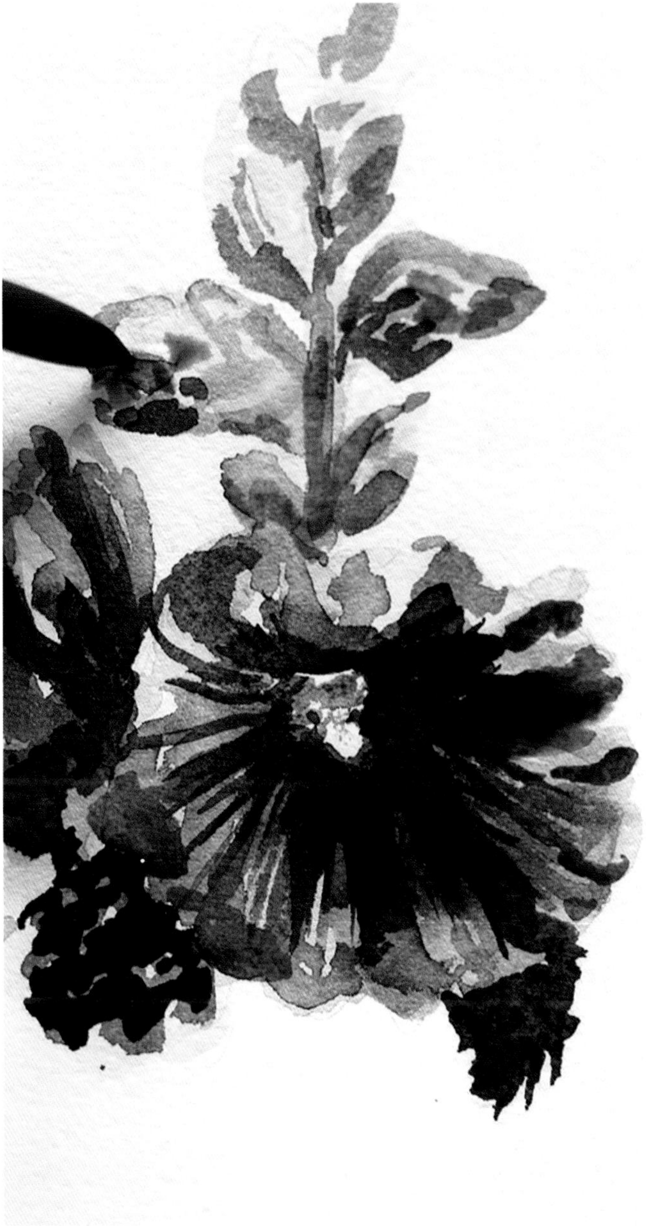

# MASTER GREENERY

*Although not as obviously varied as the vast array of colorful flowers, greenery can be just as beautiful and comes in many shapes, sizes, and shades of beautiful greens. On the following pages, I'll demonstrate several easy and simple ways to paint lovely bits of greenery that you can add to your botanical paintings to create lush, full floral artwork.*

## Leaf 1

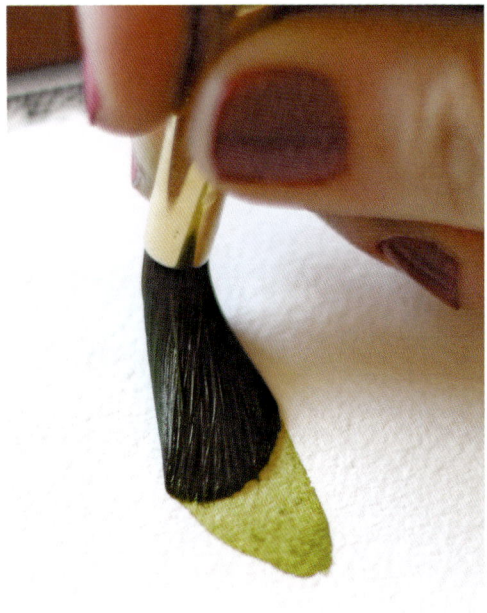
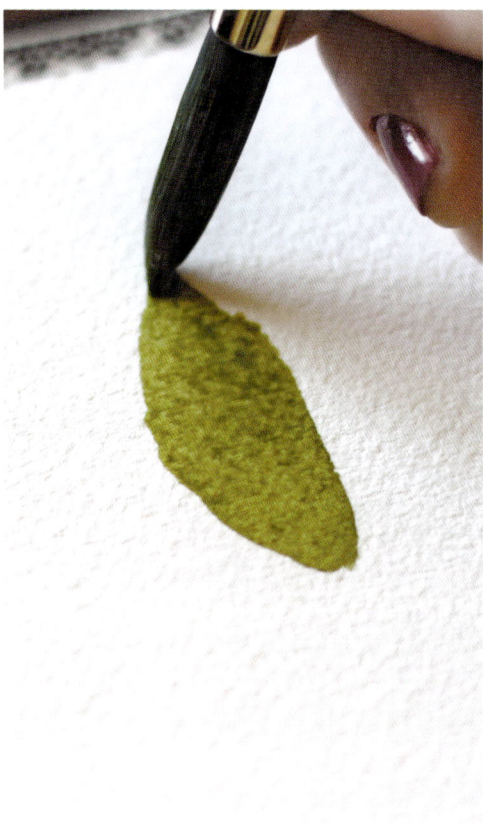

Using the body of the brush, push upward to create the entire leaf.

When you have reached the desired length of the leaf, use lighter pressure to transition to the tip of the brush to create the leaf tip.

## Leaf 2

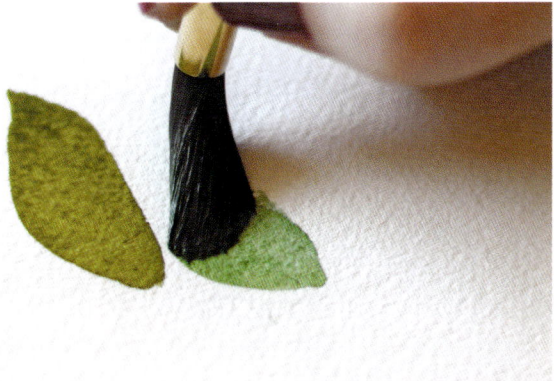

Imagining a line in the center, create a "C" shape with the body of the brush on one side.

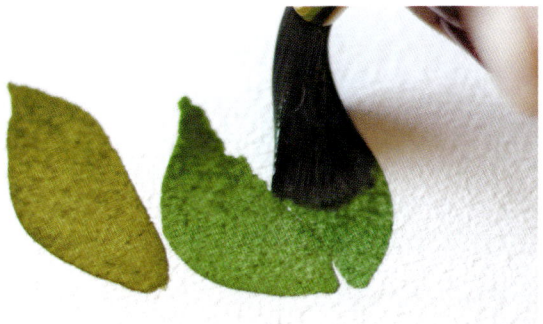

Repeat on the other side.

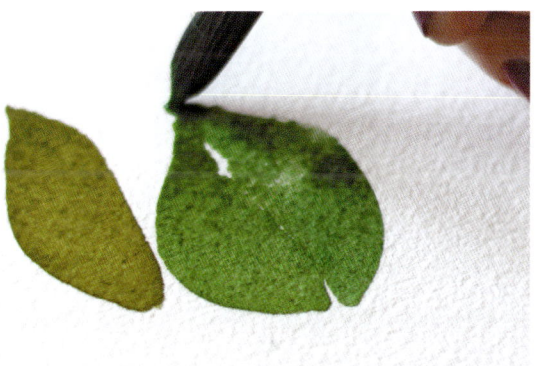

Use light pressure at the top to form the tip of the leaf.

## Leaf 3

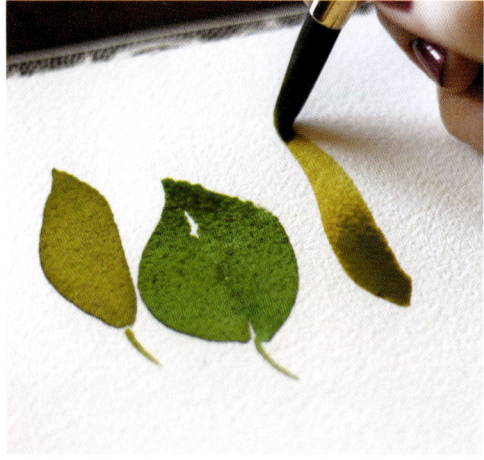 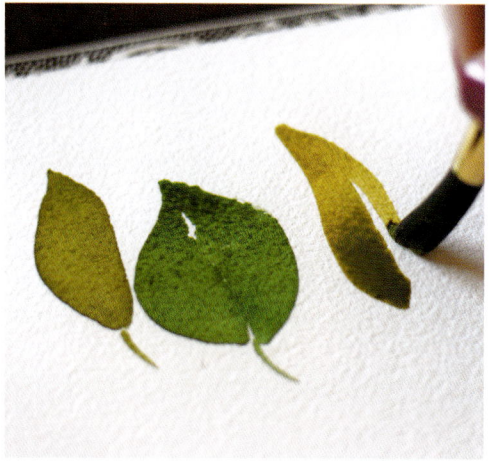

Use the body of the brush to create volume.

Paint long strokes for long leaves. Leaving the middle of the leaf white creates the illusion of a center line and defines the leaf.

## Leaf 4

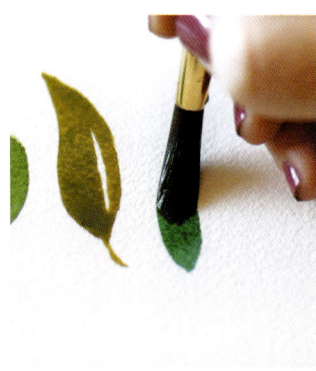 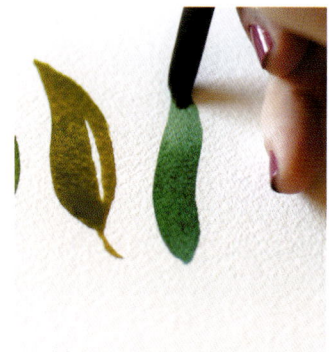 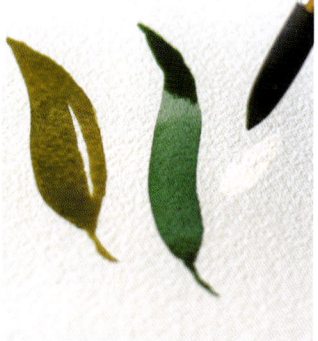

Use the body of the brush and a long stroke to create slender, elongated leaves.

Remember to decrease the pressure on the brush as you near the end of the leaf to taper the stroke.

To create depth on leaves with no center line, apply a darker color at the top or bottom— or both! This can suggest shadow, as well as new growth.

## Leaf 5

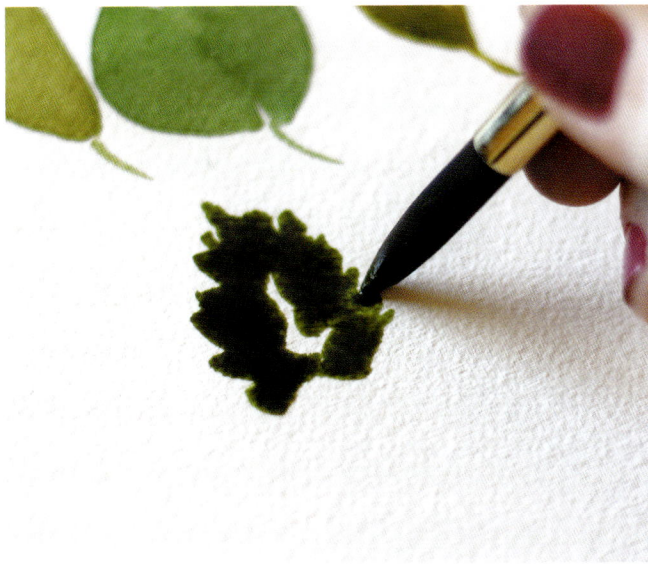

Use the tip of the brush to paint leaves with jagged or rough edges.

## Leaf 6

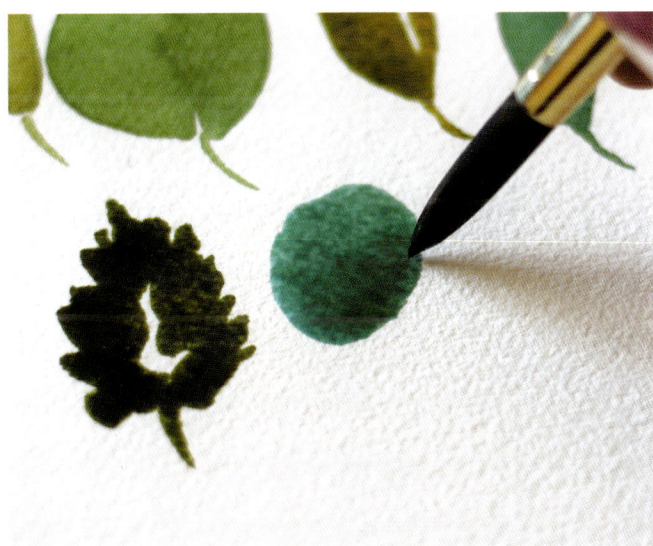

Use the body of the brush to create smooth, round leaves.

*Watercolor foliage adds stems and linework to basic leaf shapes. Building on the previous leaf prompts, master foliage as you work through six unique styles.*

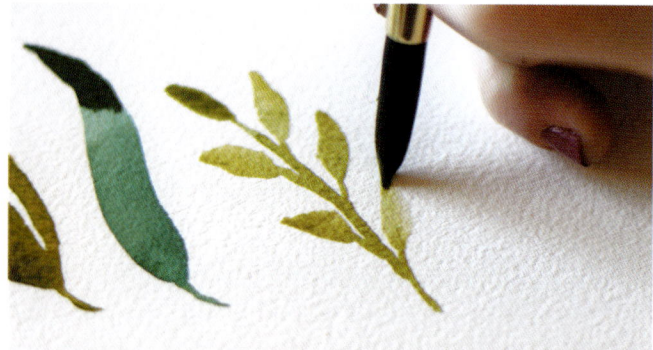

### Foliage 1

For short-leaved foliage, create the stem first. Then, use the body of the brush to paint short leaves growing from smaller stems.

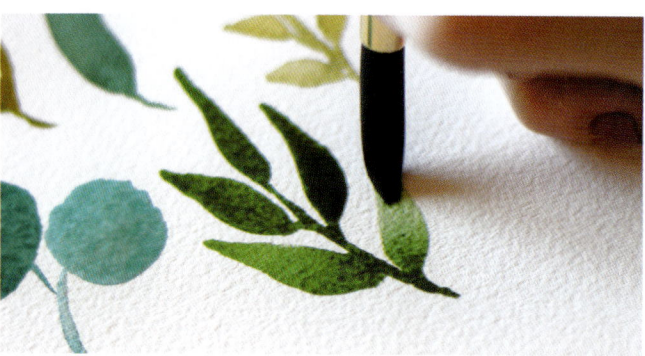

### Foliage 2

Follow the same process to paint long-leaved foliage. Create the stem first, and then use the body of the brush to paint voluminous, long leaves growing from smaller stems.

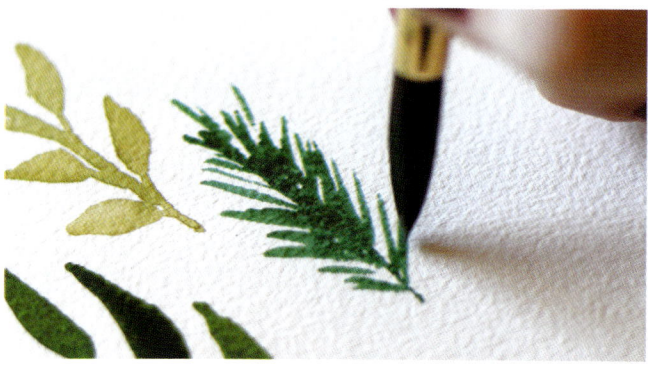

### Foliage 3

For needled foliage, use light pressure to make quick strokes outward from the stem with the brush tip.

### Foliage 4

Make long strokes for longer needles. For rounded needle tips, start away from the center and bring the point of the brush to the stems.

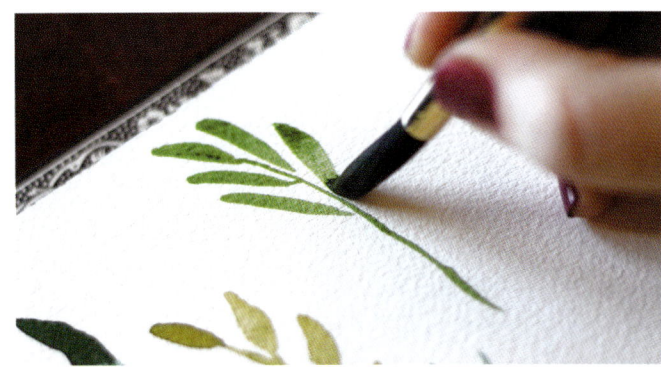

### Foliage 5

Stems and random shapes perfectly capture the look of scattered greens, such as weeds.

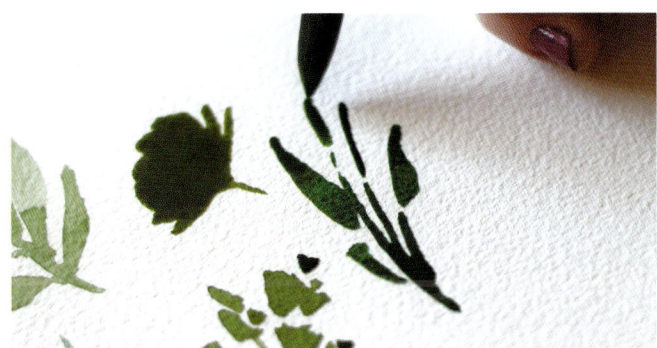

### Foliage 6

When painting grass, create long, thin lines while altering the direction they point.

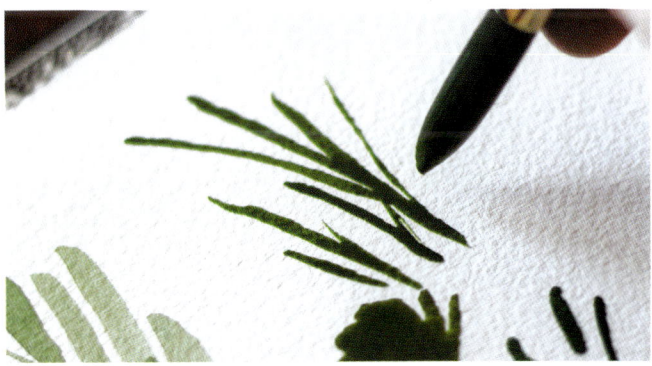

PAINT A CACTUS

*Long lines with white space in between perfectly capture the spines on a saguaro cactus.*

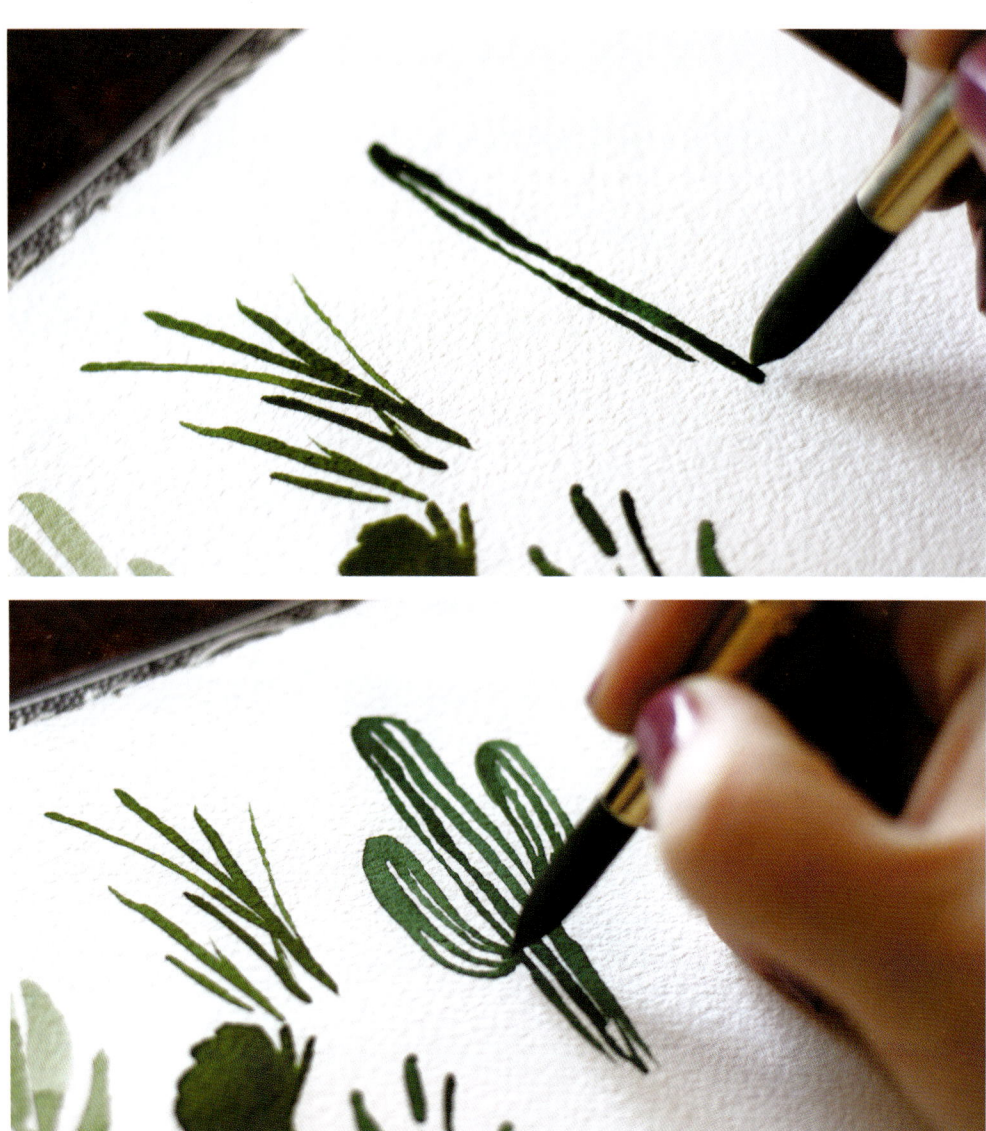

PAINT A FERN

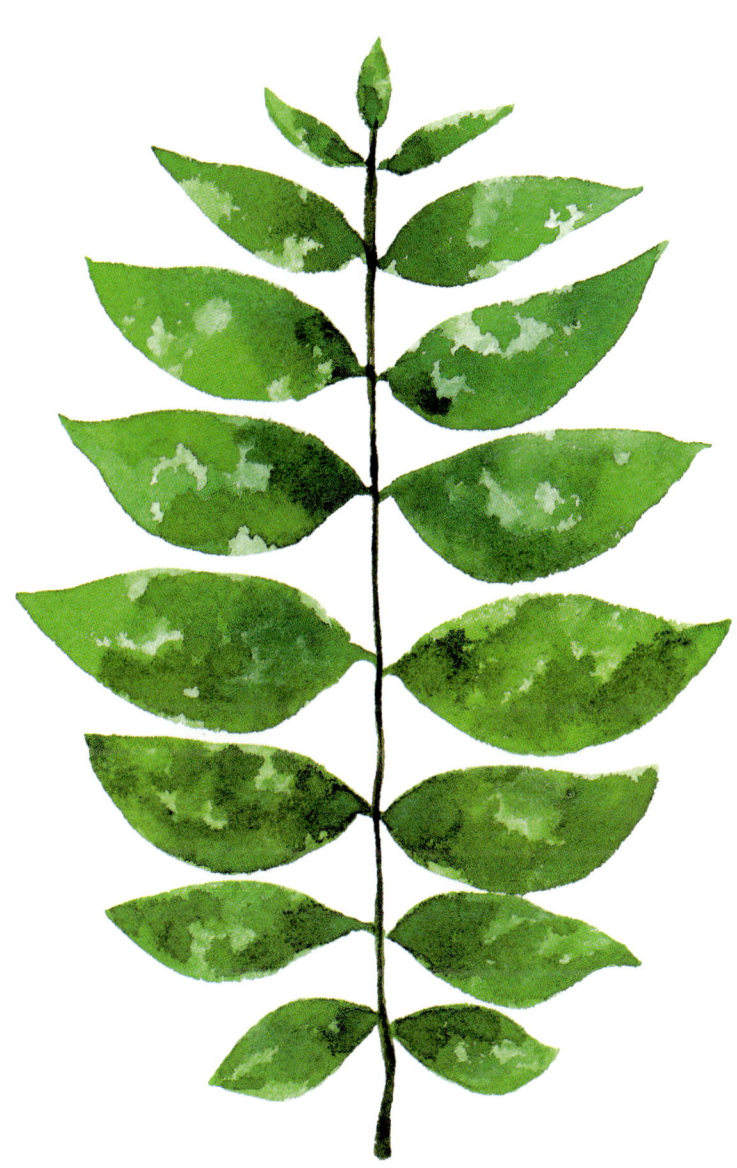

# WATERCOLOR A WREATH

*Wreaths are fun and easy to paint. They make very pretty, simple stand-alone art. They can also be used as frames for watercolor lettering, an initial, or a monogram!*

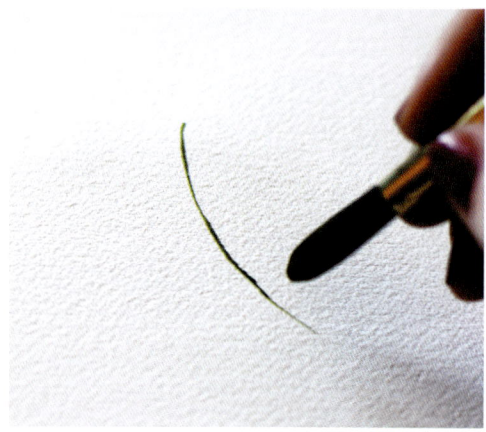

Start with the "bones" of the wreath—the stems.

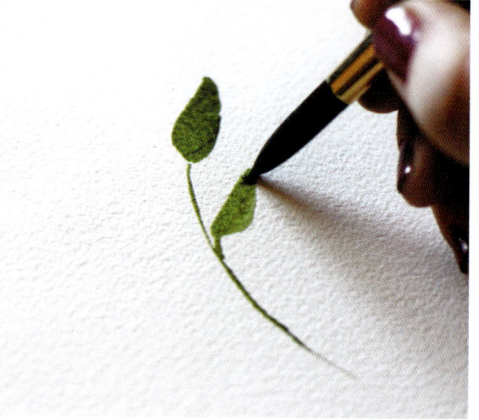

Begin placing leaves with a medium-light color value.

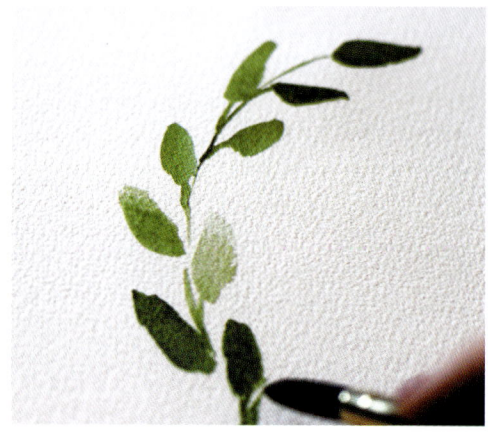

Continue adding leaves, alternating on each side of the stem.

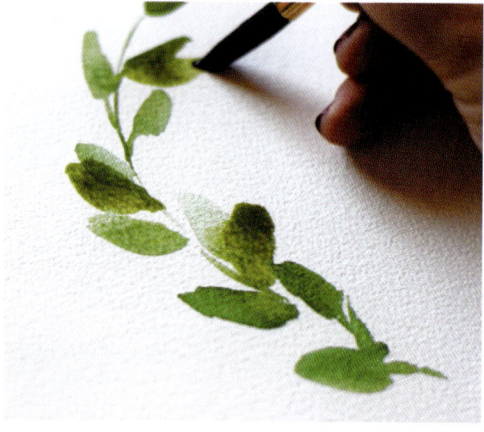

Next, add another color hue. Use either a darker shade of the first color or another hue for variation and contrast.

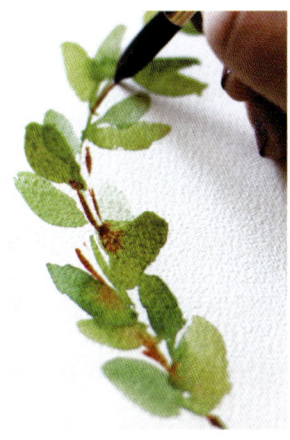 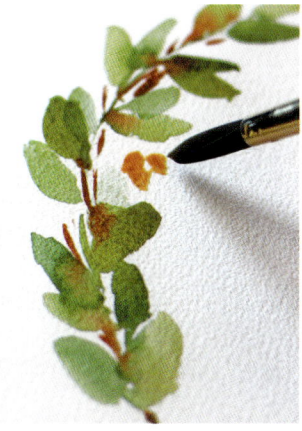 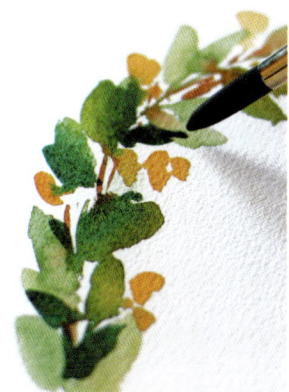

Add a highly contrasting color for balance. This red-brown is the complementary color of green and tones down the green hues while providing interest.

Add flowers to the wreath.

Add even darker greenery for contrast.

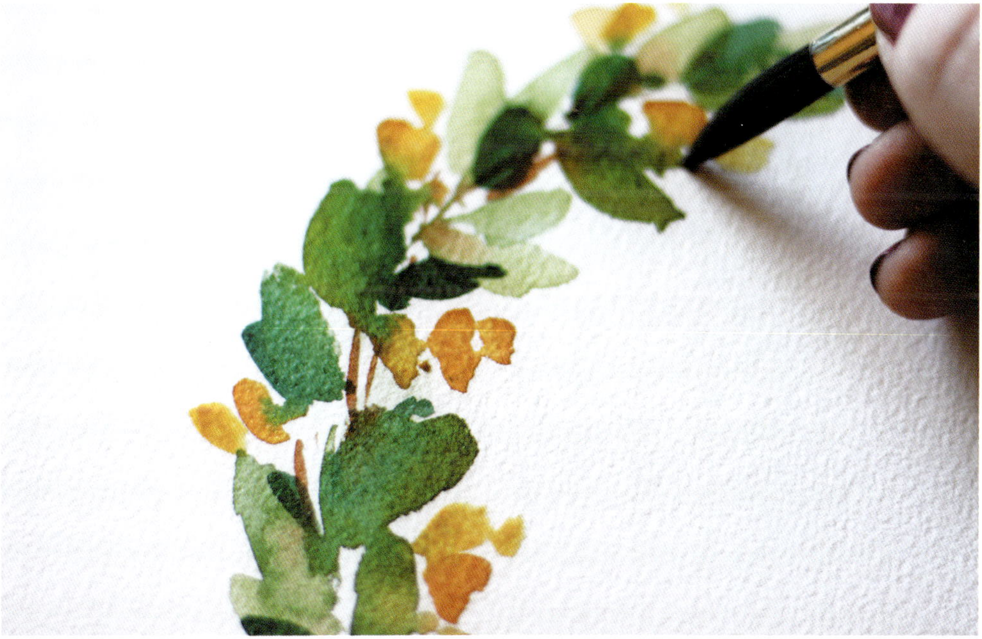

*Experiment with adding layers of color from lightest to darkest to make a wreath with depth.*

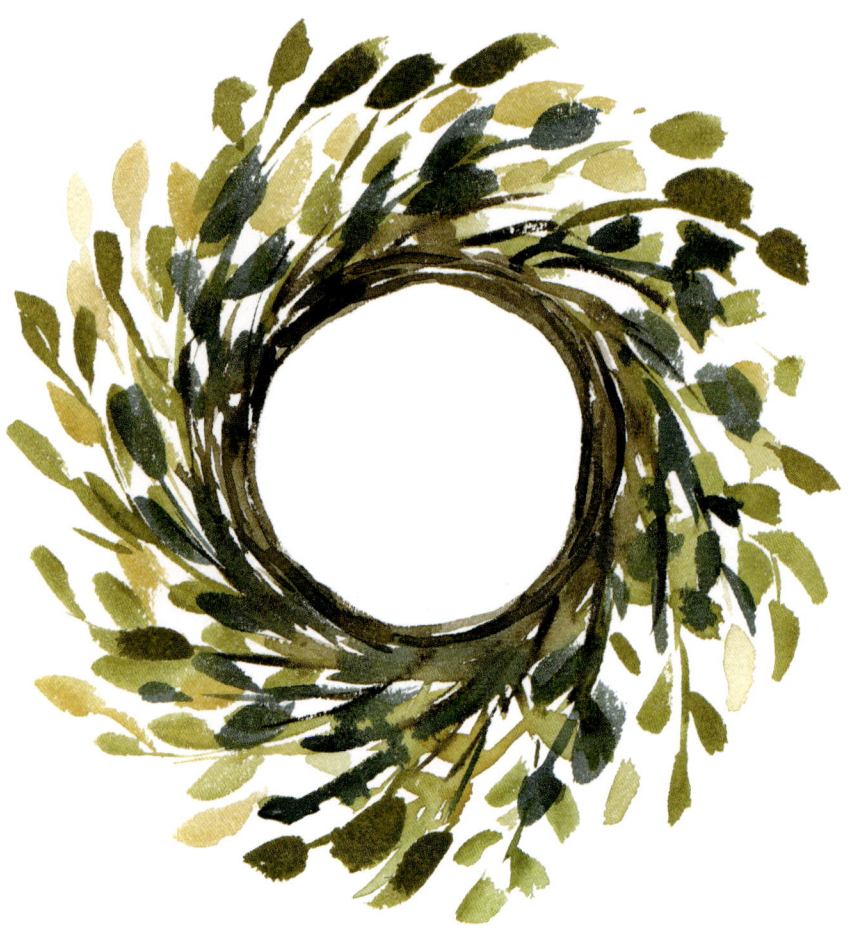

**40** PAINT A SPRING WREATH

*Find inspiration each season and paint a wreath with flowers that bloom in winter, spring, summer, and fall.*

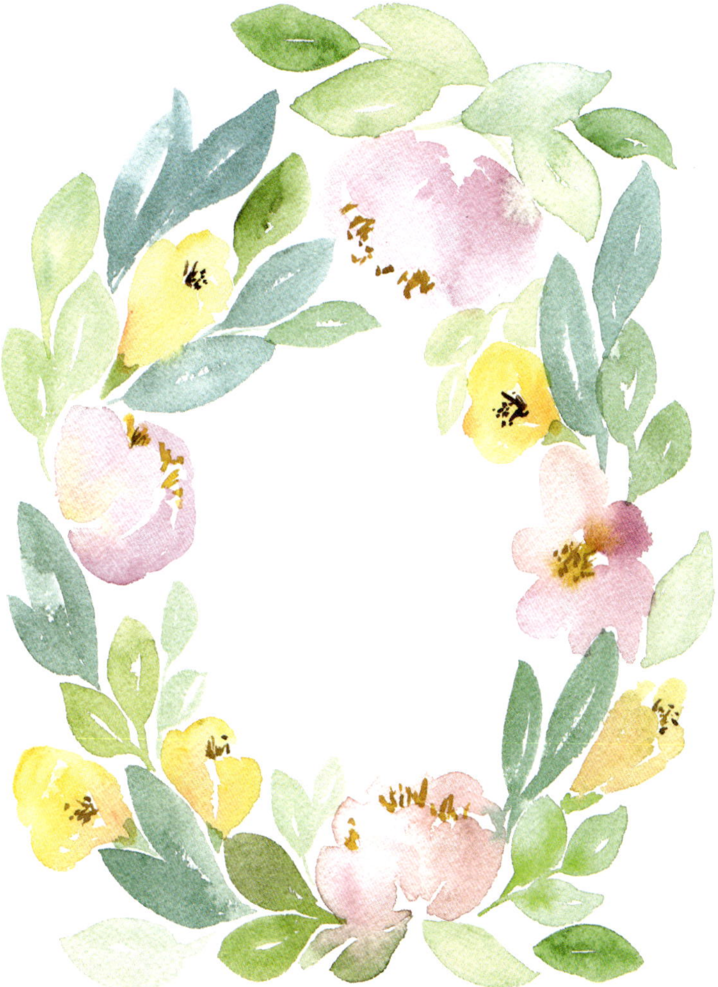

# CREATE AN ALLOVER PATTERN

*Once you've mastered painting botanicals, try piecing them together to create pretty patterns.*

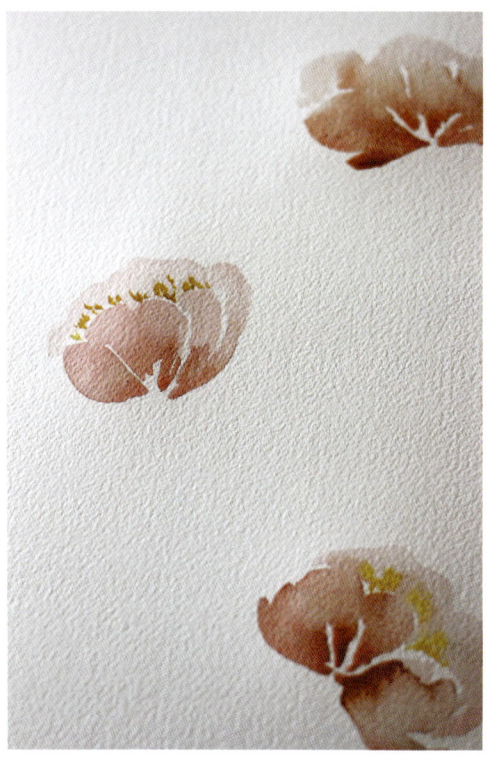

Start with the focus of the pattern. Here, I began with pink peonies. Scatter them in whatever way is pleasing to you and fulfills the point of the pattern.

Paint the first layer of leaves or foliage. This is the base color for the pattern—not too light and not too dark.

Add a secondary floral to support the main floral. It should be different in shape and ideally different in color.

Add darker leaves. This will be the darkest value in the pattern. Add enough leaves to create high contrast with the rest of the elements, but not so many that it overwhelms the flow.

**CONTINUED**

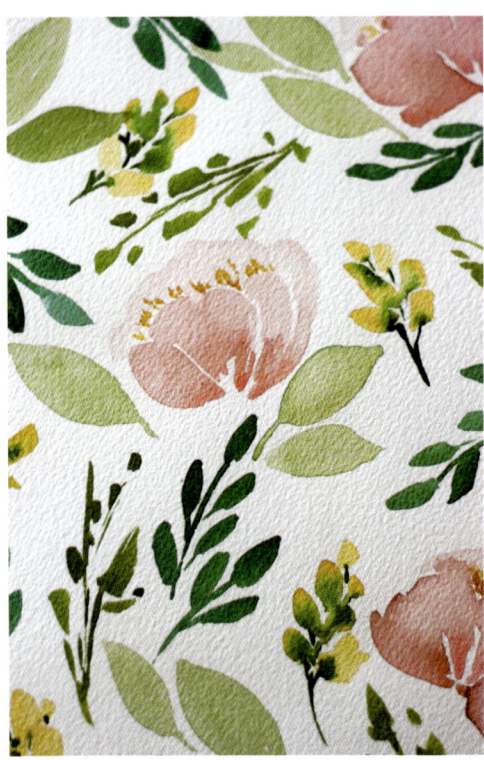

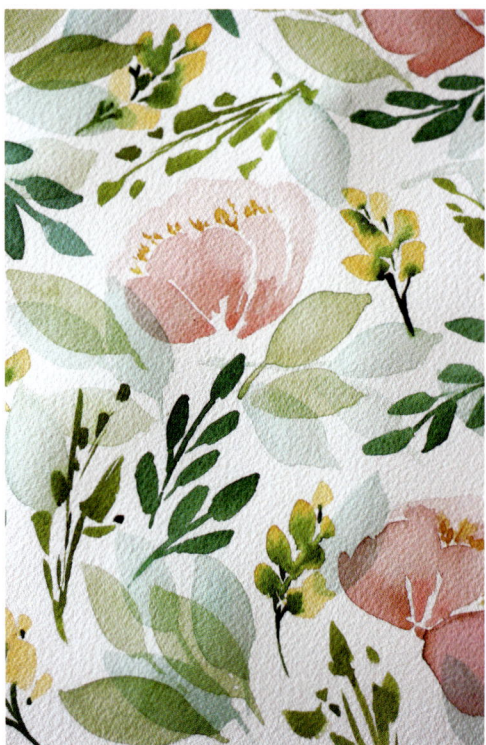

Add a textured element, such as grass or weeds—something with movement that isn't as uniform. This will break up the pattern and keep it from looking too stiff.

Once everything is dry, add another element in a very light wash. Overlap the different elements to connect them together. This last step isn't necessary, but it usually gives the pattern a feeling of completion.

# PLAY WITH COLOR IN PATTERN

*Create an allover floral pattern with flowers in red, orange, yellow, blue, and purple.*

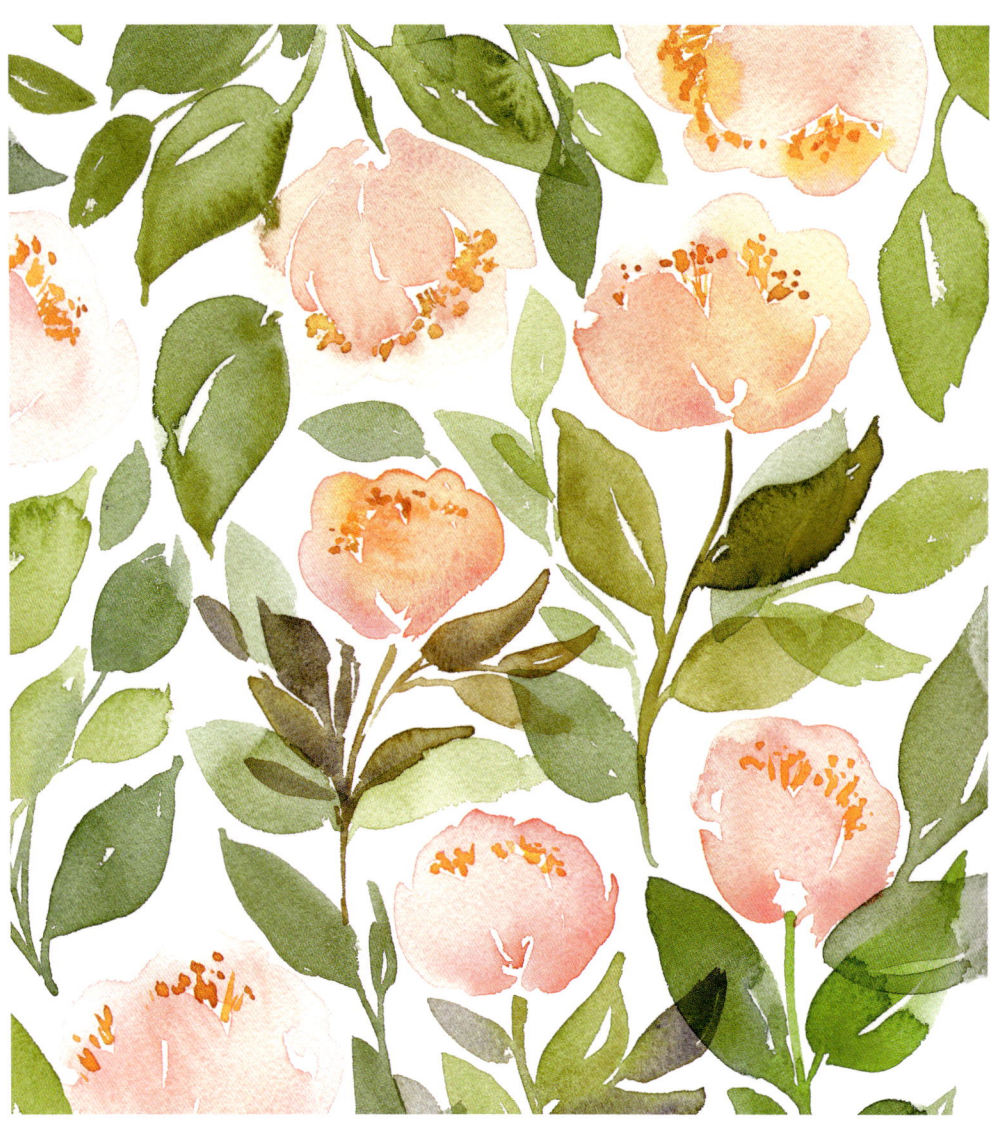

# FILL A PAGE WITH ROSES

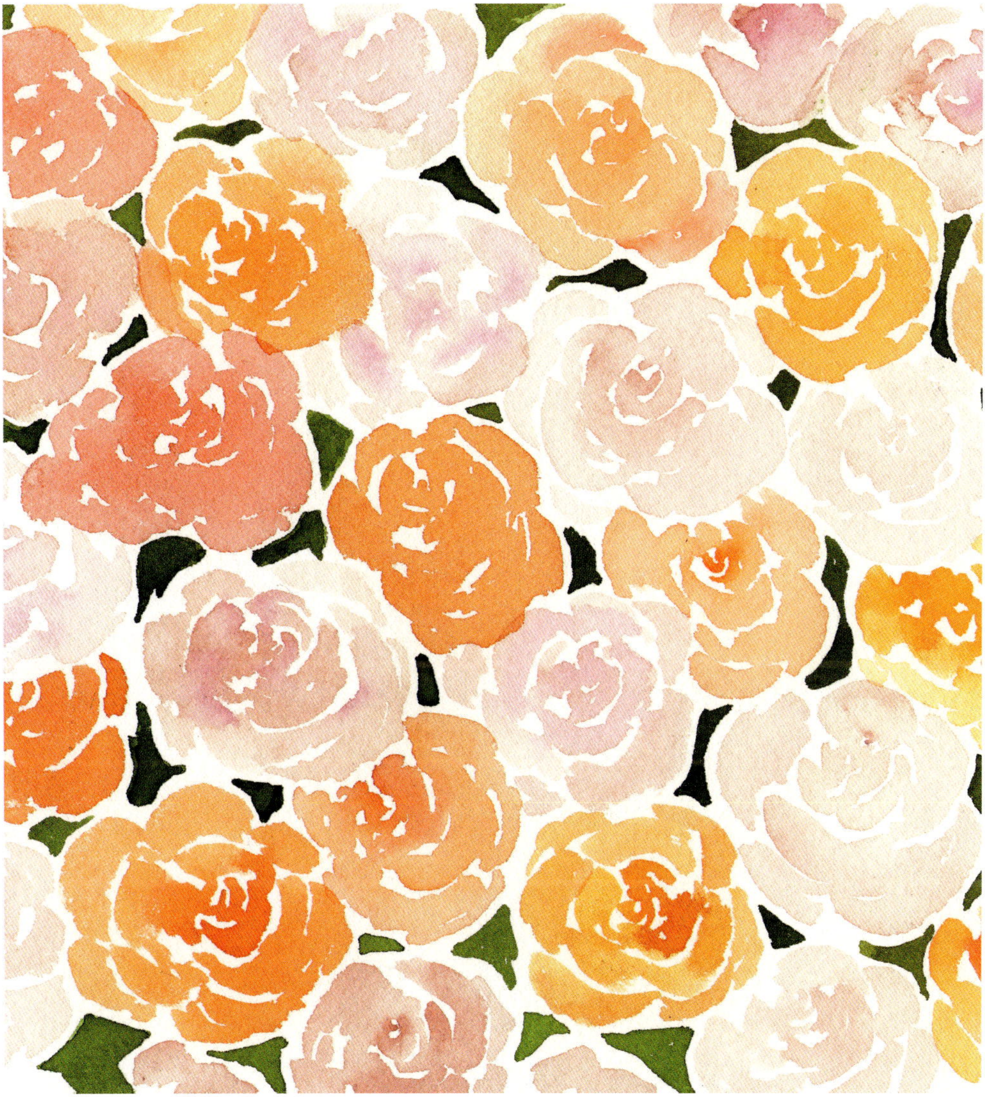

# PAINT A FOX

*Animals make great subject matter for watercolor painting. You don't need to add a lot of detail to paint your favorite critters. Just start with a quick pencil sketch, and then use simple strokes and add a few fine details—the human eye fills in the rest. These next few prompts guide you through painting some cute furry and feathered friends.*

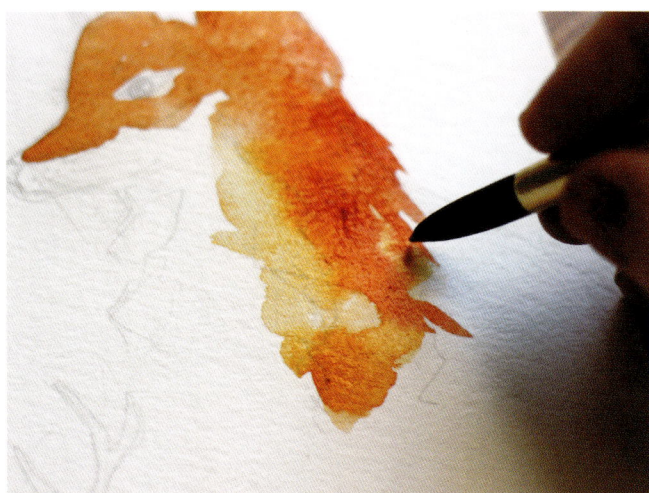

Apply a light wash of orange watercolor paint evenly on dry paper, leaving the white parts of the fur unpainted. While the paint is wet, drop in bright yellow, red, and orange to create interest and variety.

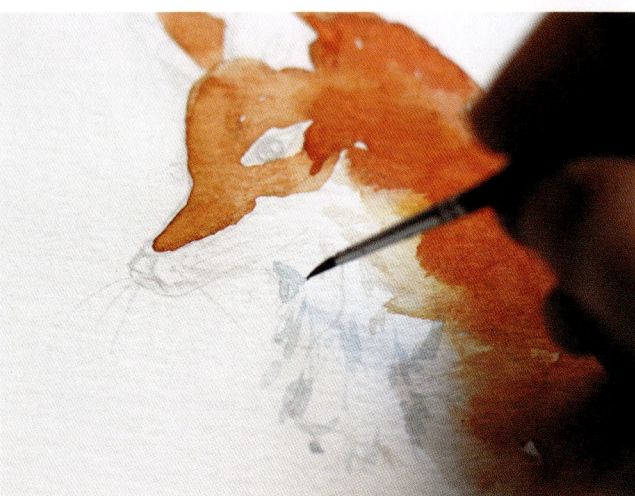

Paint fur details on the white areas with light gray paint to add depth. Don't overdo it— you only need to create the impression of fur, not paint each individual hair.

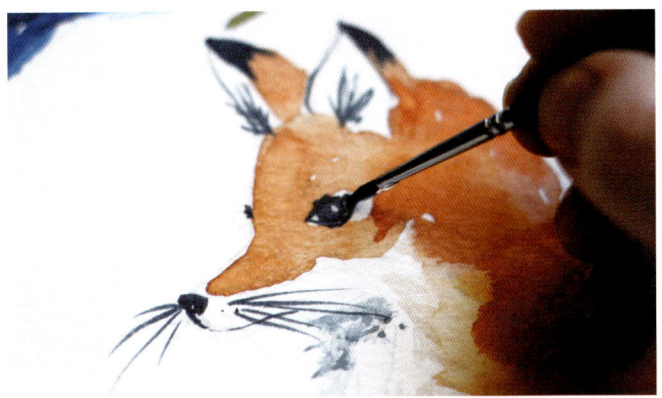

Use black paint for the nose and mouth, eyes, whiskers, and inner ear hair detail Paint the tips of the ears black. Dilute black paint with water to lighten, and add a shadow under the chin to add dimension, as well as a few strokes in the chest fur.

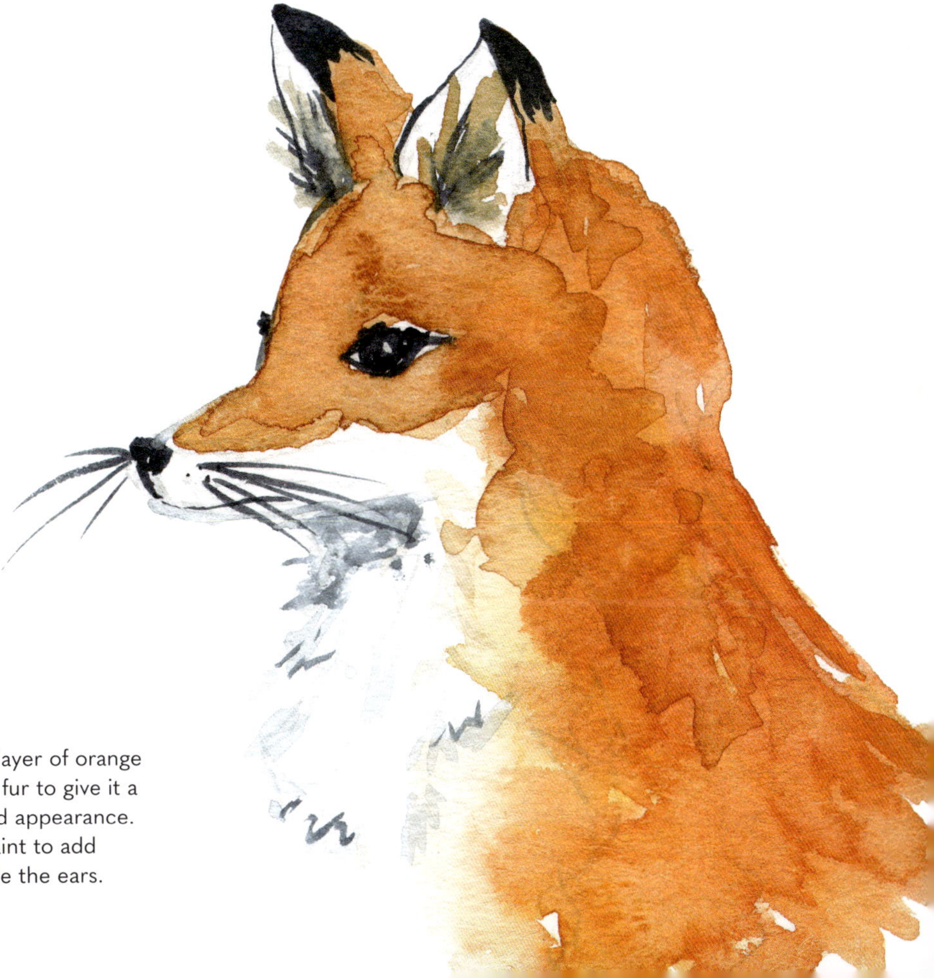

Add another layer of orange over the fox's fur to give it a fuller, textured appearance. Use brown paint to add shadows inside the ears.

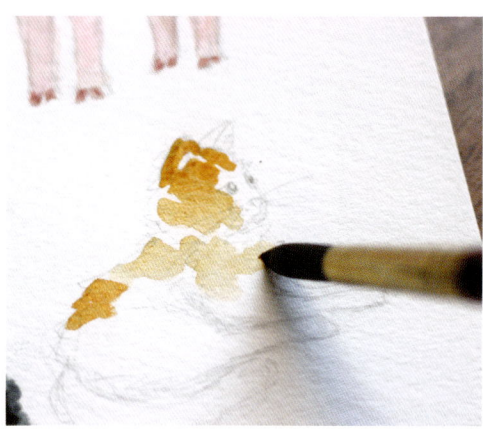

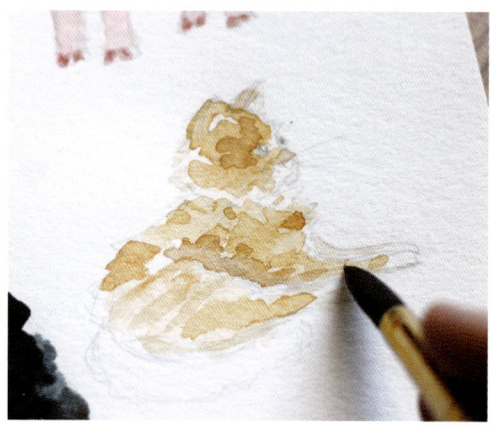

Paint patches of orange watercolor to start the cat's fur. This cat also has patches of white fur, so keep a lot of white space for contrast.

Add more defined patches and stripes by adding a darker orange shade. Remember that you can't add white and light colors back in, so be light-handed when adding darker colors.

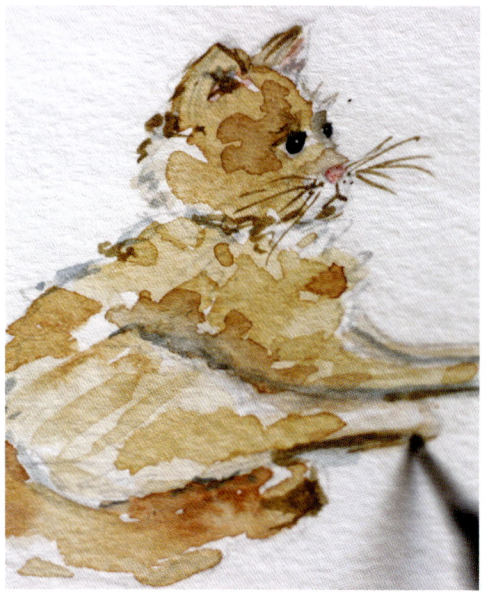

Add nose, mouth, whiskers, and eye details. Apply darker brown fur to define the legs, head, ears, and tail. Then, use light gray paint to define areas of the white fur.

Notice how my illustration of a cat is truly nothing more than some simple brushstrokes and variation in color value to create depth. You don't need to consider yourself an artist to work with watercolor paints. Anyone can create simple paintings!

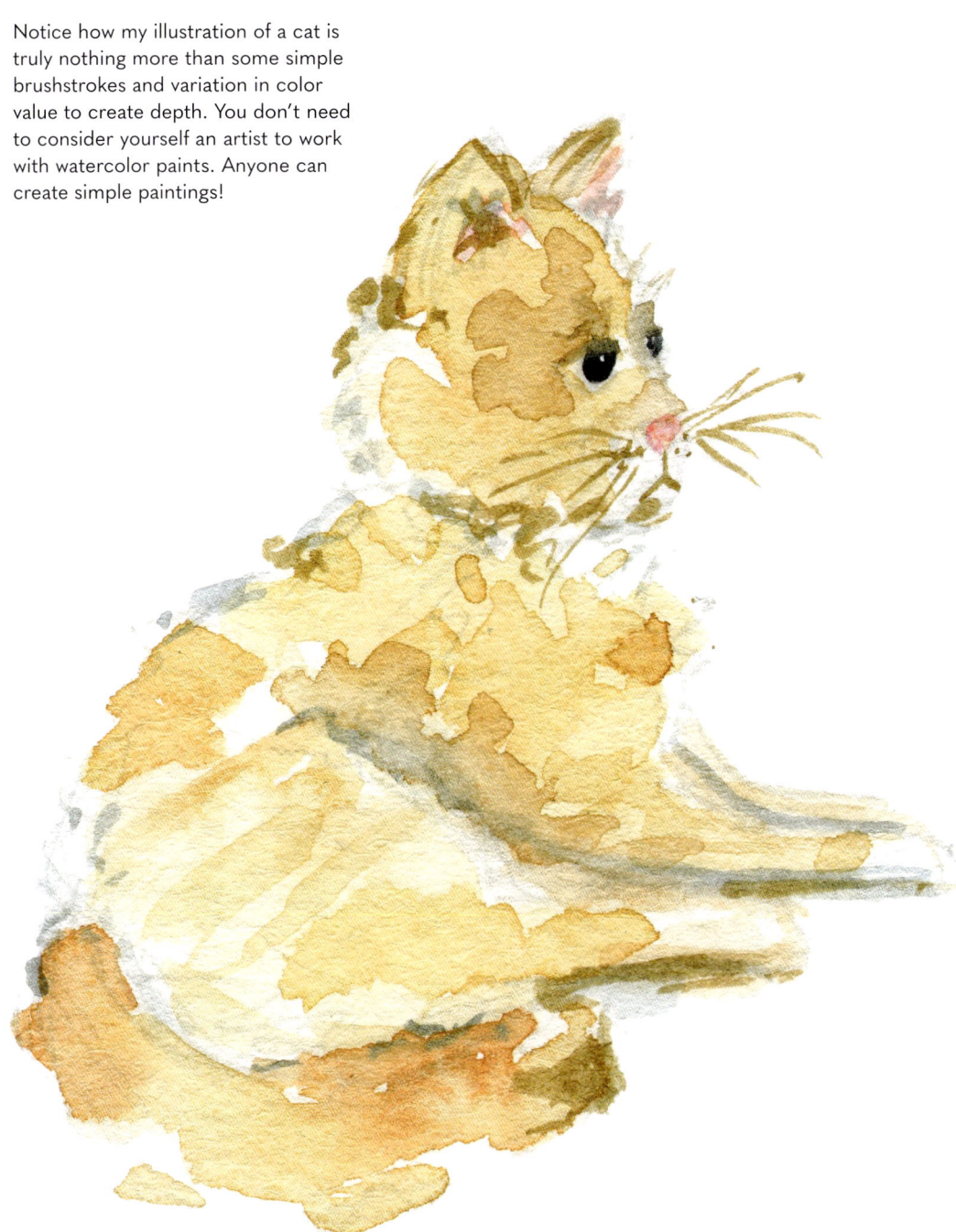

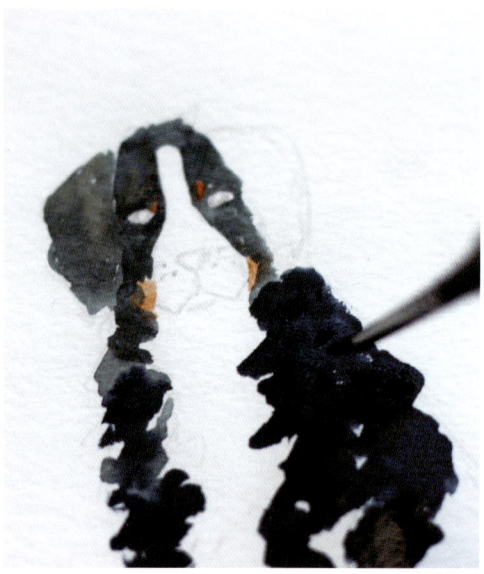

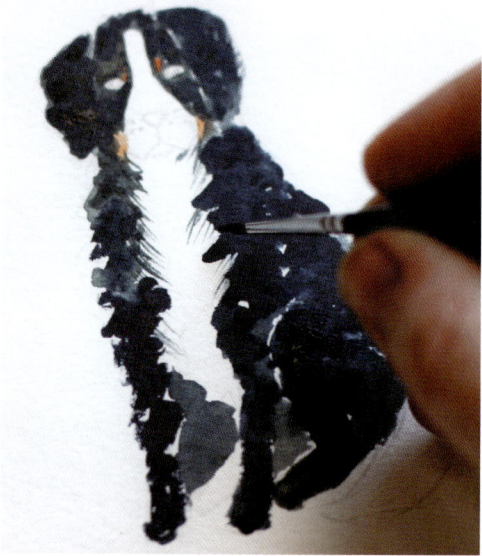

First, paint tiny eyebrows and a touch of brown on the sides of the face. Then, paint the black body, applying the paint unevenly and in layers to mimic the texture of dog fur. Leave white areas of fur unpainted.

Bring black into the chest to define the edges of the white fur, making light, sweeping brushstrokes from the black paint into the chest.

Add nose, mouth, and eye details. Use light gray paint to define the white fur at the mouth and chest.

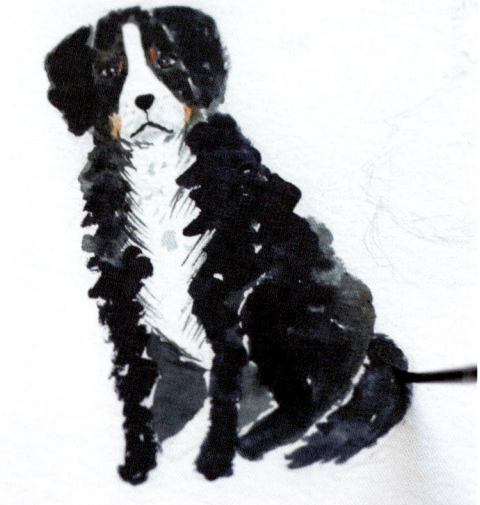

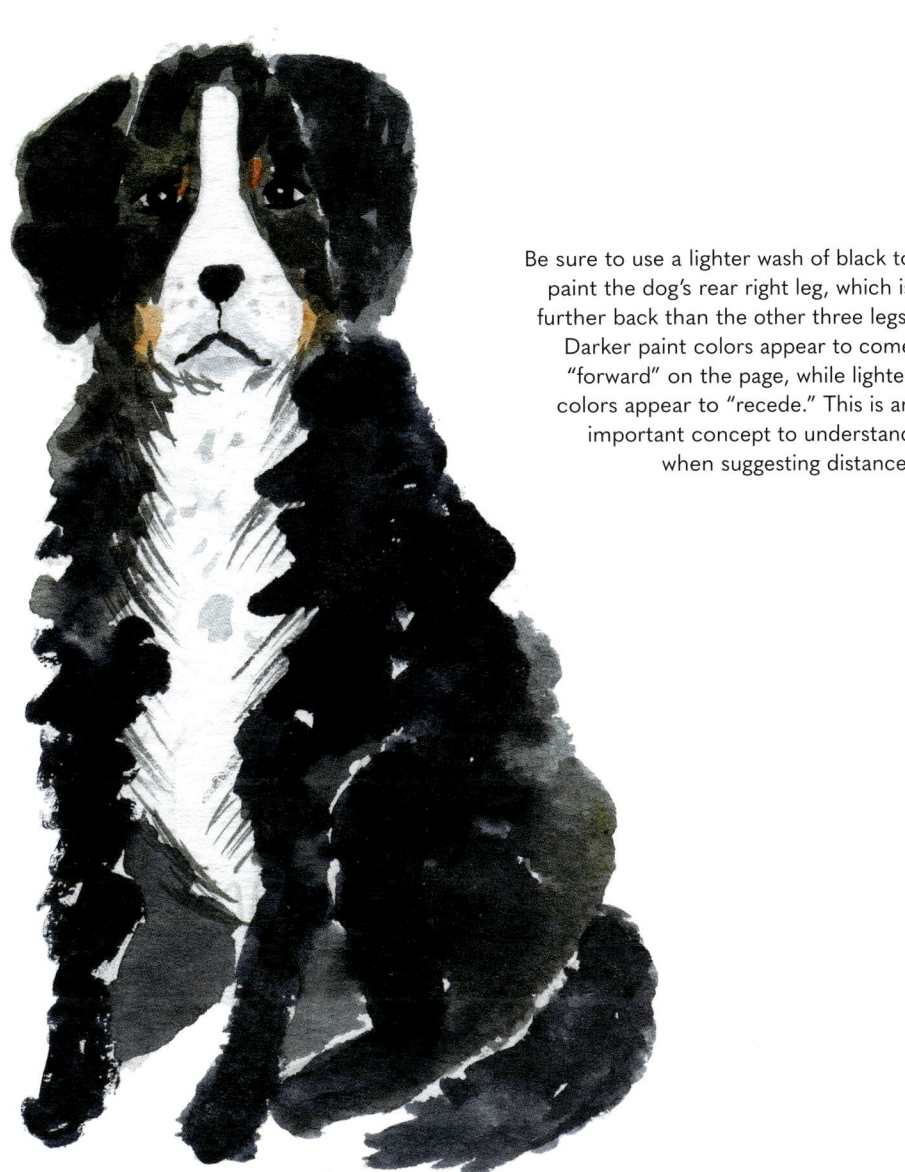

Be sure to use a lighter wash of black to paint the dog's rear right leg, which is further back than the other three legs. Darker paint colors appear to come "forward" on the page, while lighter colors appear to "recede." This is an important concept to understand when suggesting distance.

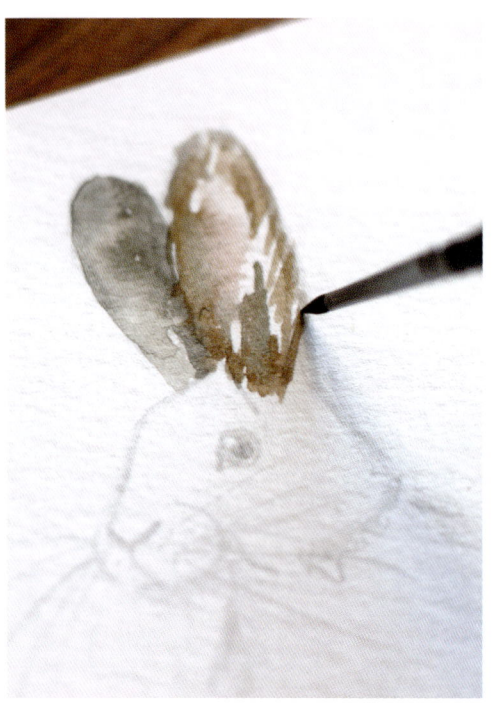 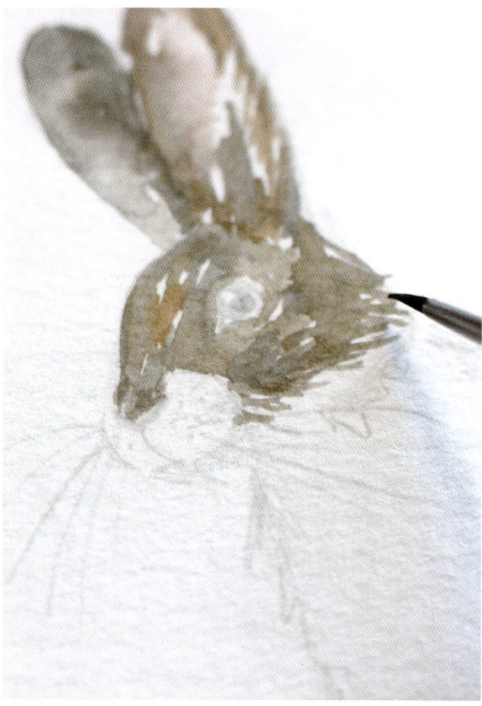

Start by painting the rabbit's ears and working down the body. The fur is very textured; use patchy, thin strokes.

Rabbit fur has a lot of dimension and color. Use shades of gray and brown to achieve the look, leaving any white areas unpainted. Paint the thin fur strokes in the direction of growth.

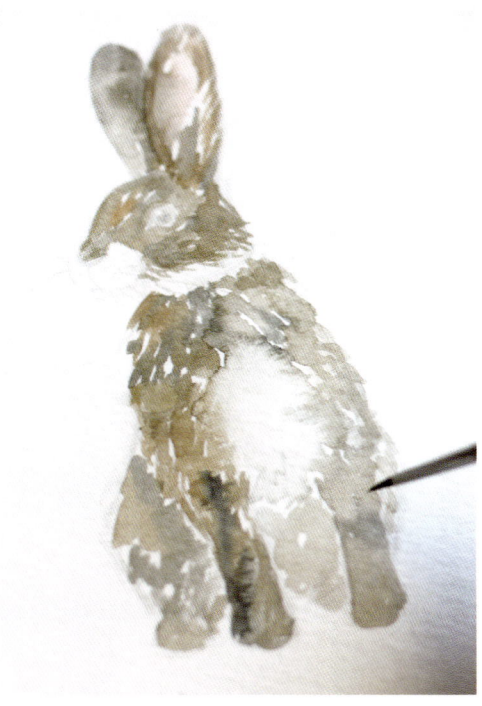

Add nose, mouth, whiskers, and eye details. Apply darker brown fur to define the legs, head, ears, and tail. Then, use light gray paint to define areas of the white fur.

Add nose, mouth, whisker, and eye details. Use light gray to define the white and light areas of fur.

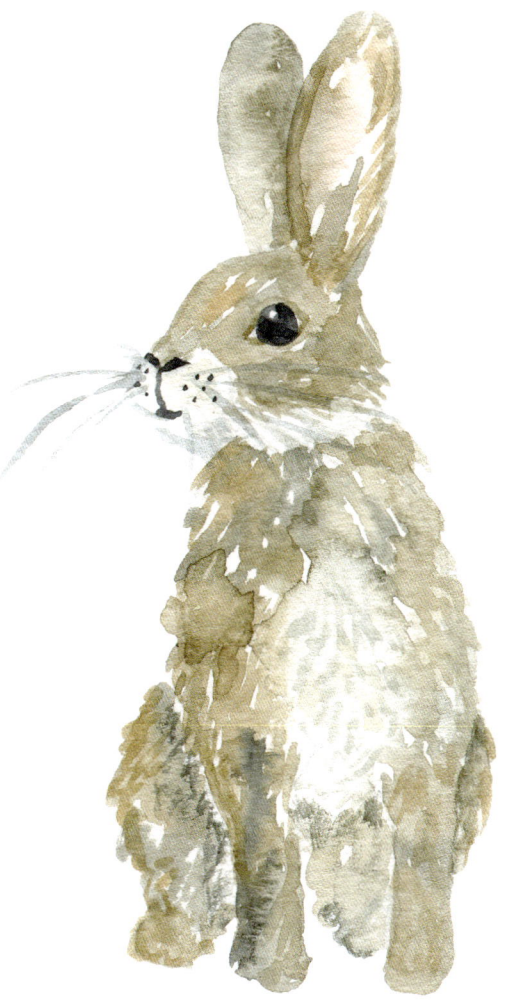

# PAINT A SQUIRREL

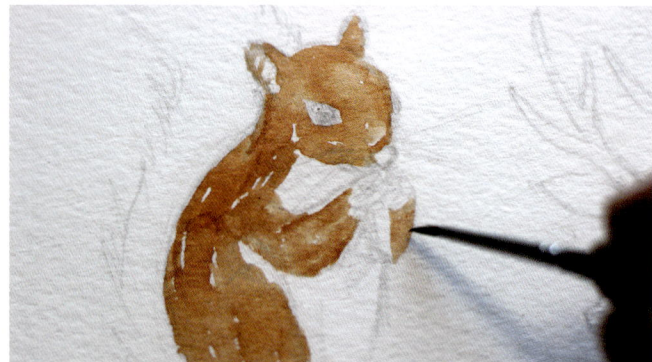

Apply a light brown wash of watercolor across the body, leaving the white of the paper for the white fur. Leave a few small unpainted areas in the brown fur for highlights.

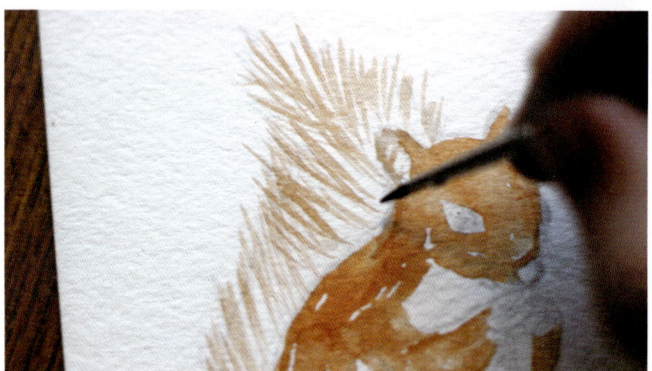

Squirrel tails are darker at the center and lighter at the edges—an important observation since you need to start with the lighter color first. Use light, sweeping strokes going out from the body of the squirrel.

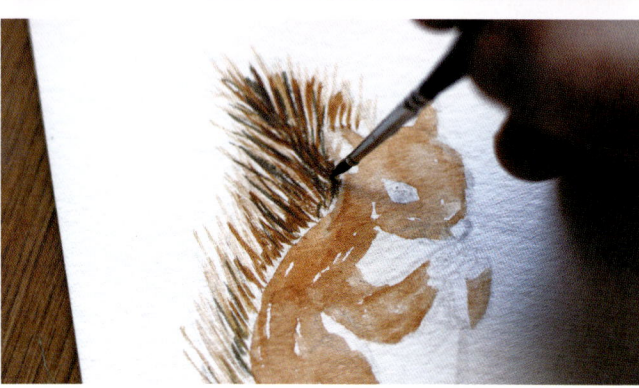

Progressively add darker and darker browns until you are satisfied with the darkest hue. Remember that you can't add back white or lighter tones, so add dark colors sparingly.

Use black to paint the nose, mouth, and whiskers, as well as the eyes and a few dark accents. Paint gray details and shadows on the white fur. For added texture, apply another layer of color over the brown fur.

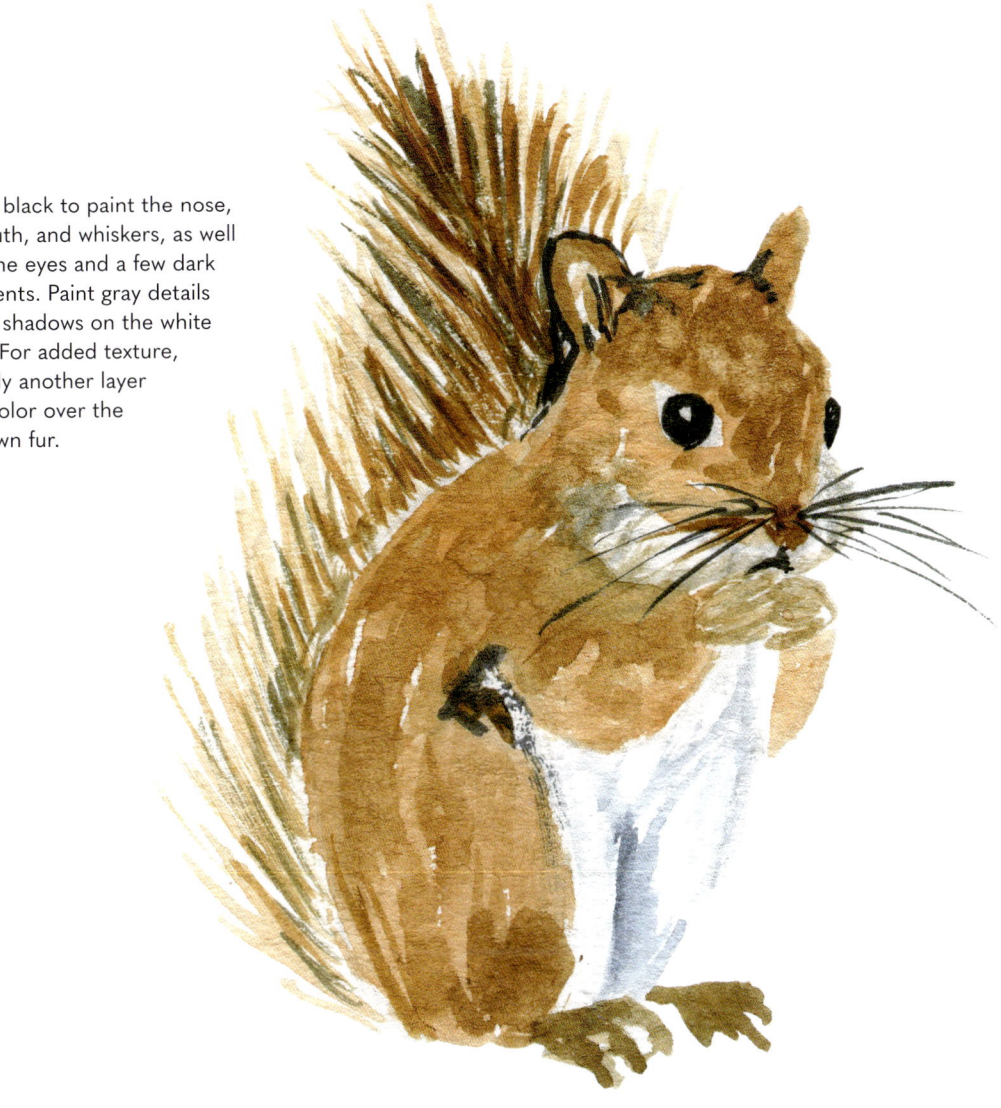

# PAINT A CHICKEN

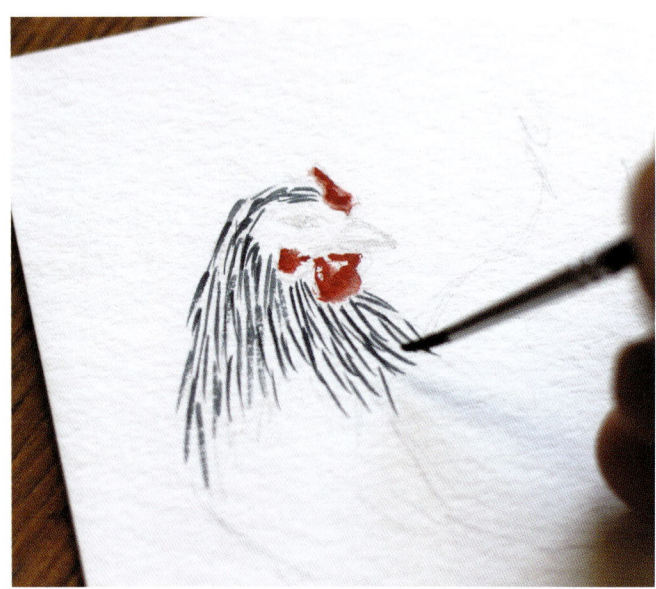

Start by painting the red areas on the chicken's head. Leave small areas of white for highlights. Use a small detail brush to paint small strokes in the direction of the feathers. This breed has long black-and-white neck feathers. Leave lots of white space for the white feathers.

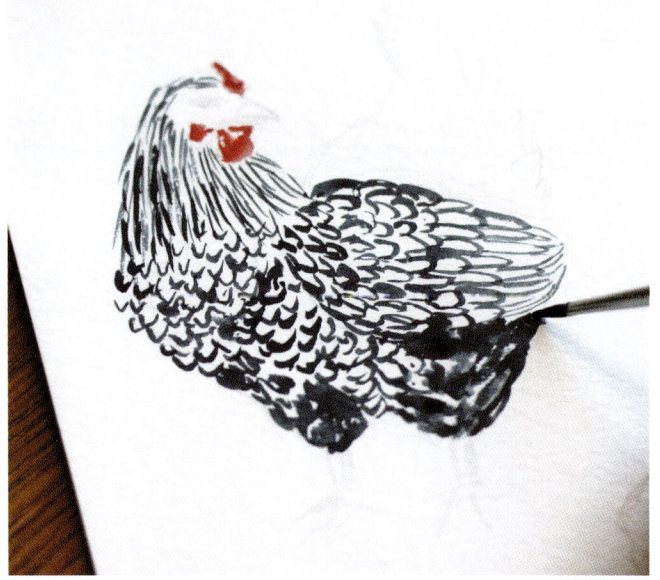

Paint small scallop shapes on the breast and wings. Define the wings from the body by making the feathers slightly longer and linear. Paint the leg feathers darker and closer together, showing less white. Use long, tapering strokes to paint the feathers at the tip of the wing.

Finish off the feathers along
the tail, fanning them out.
Add details to the feet,
beak, and eyes.

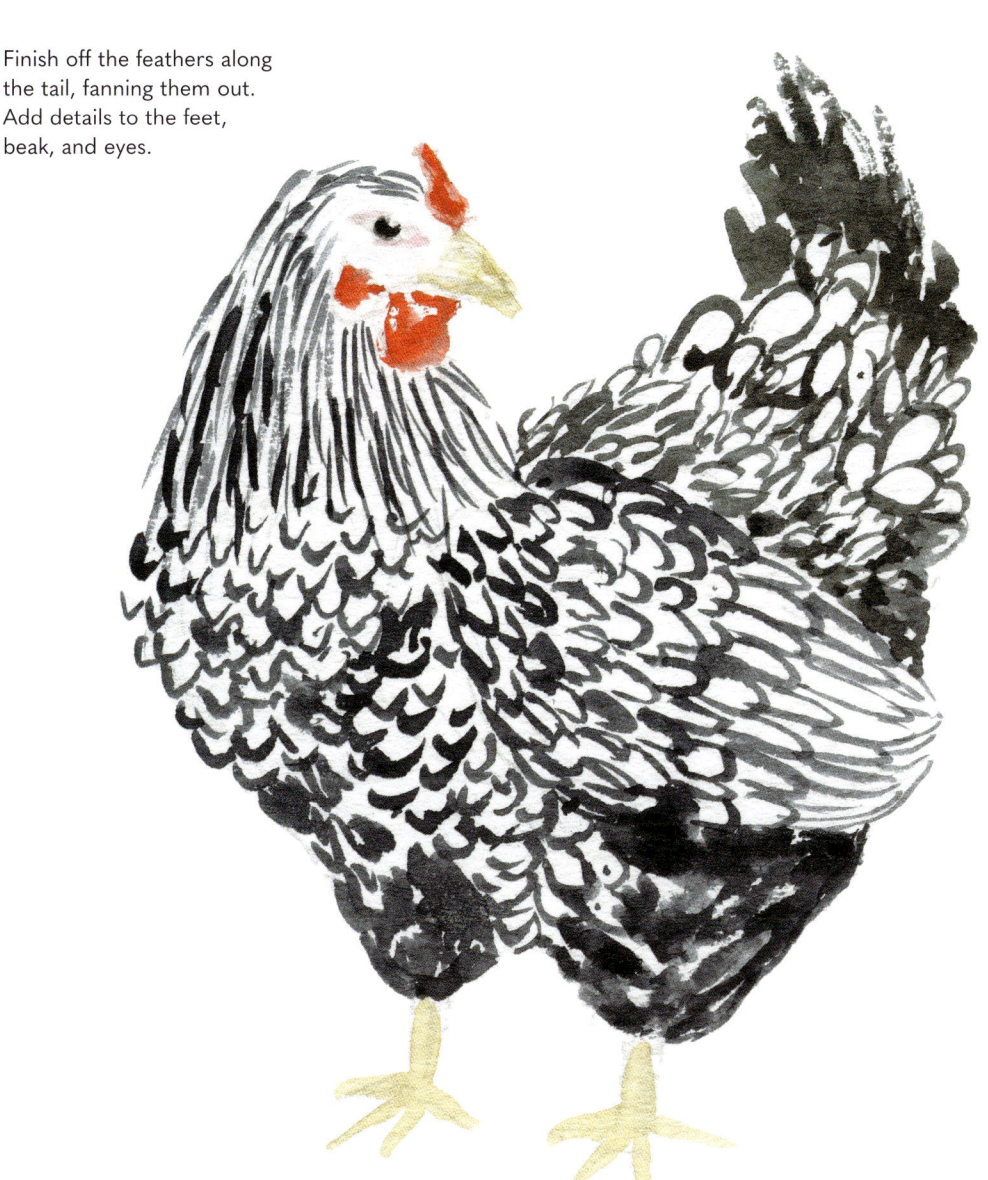

PAINT A PIG

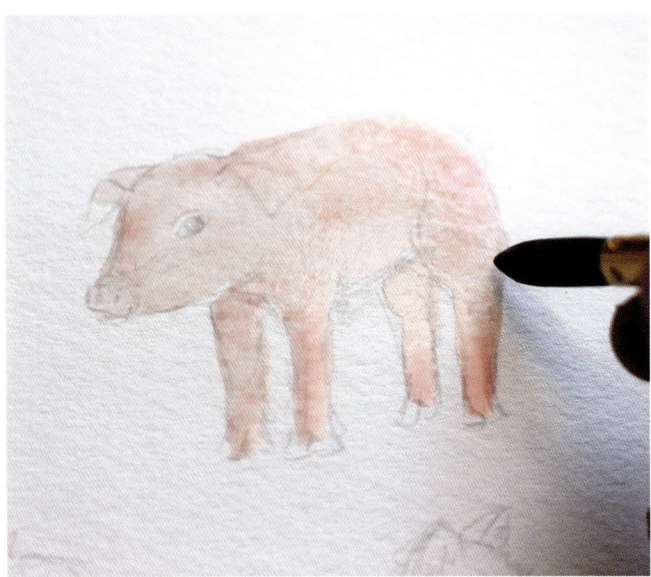

Start by painting an initial light layer of pink watercolor over the pig's body.

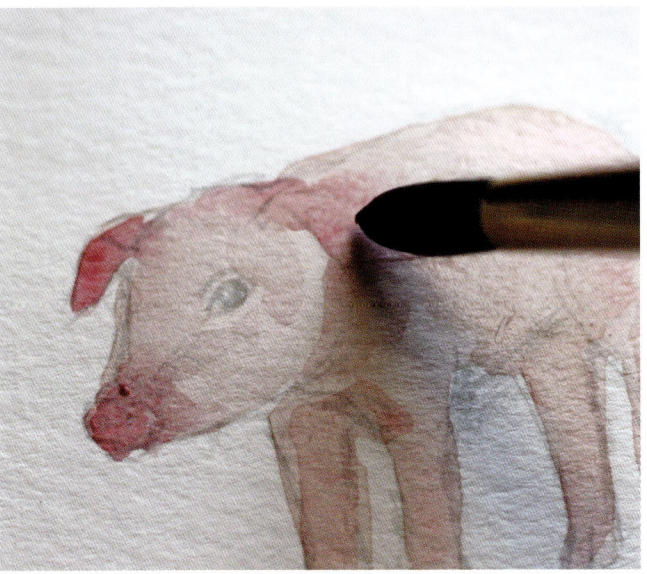

Add detail to the nose, eye, and hoofs. Create wrinkle lines around the eyes and nose with a slightly darker pink. Just a few lines will do the trick!

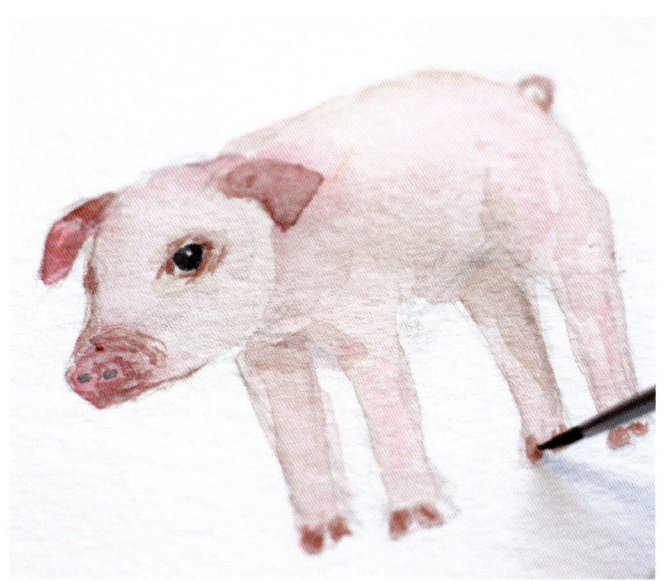

Add a more concentrated pink shade to the ears and nose to create dimension. Add another layer of light pink to the body for texture and depth.

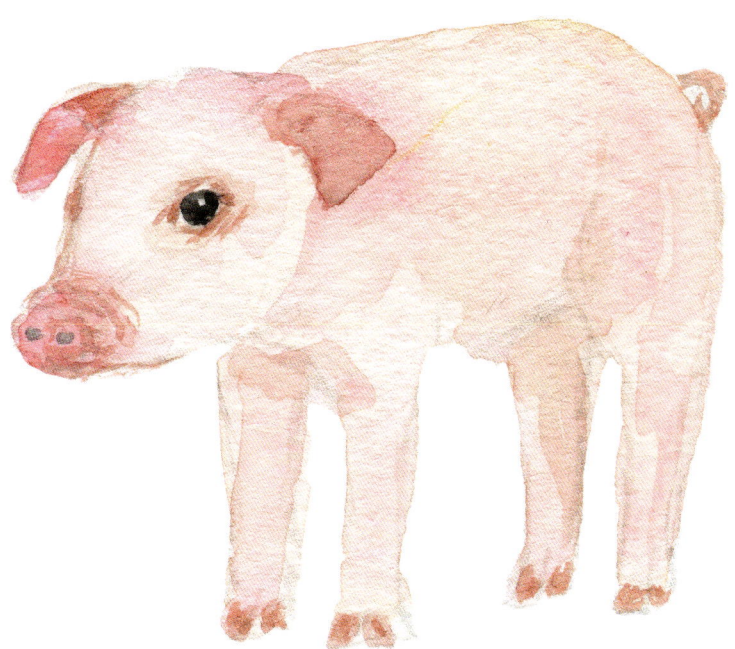

# PAINT A BUTTERFLY

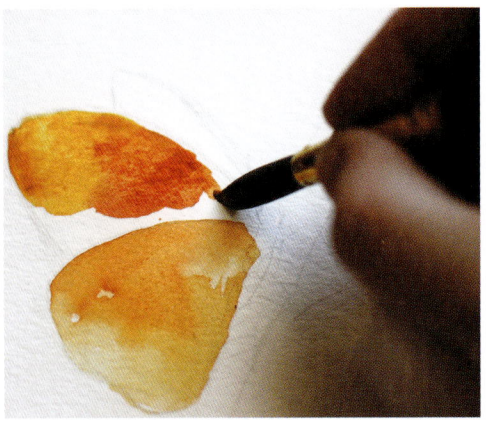

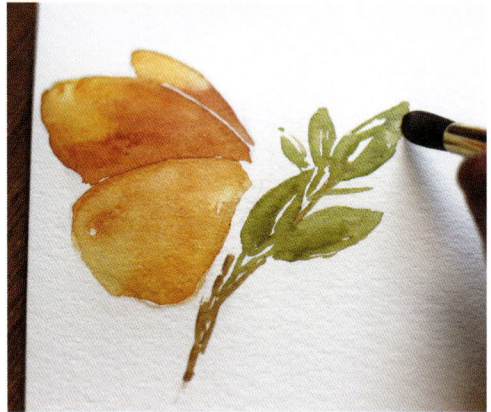

Start with the base layer of watercolor paint. Use different shades of orange and yellow for interest.

While the wings dry, paint the leaves, flowers, or branches. You should paint this early on so that it can dry before you paint the butterfly's body and legs.

Add line detail on the wings with black paint, using light pressure for the thin strokes and heavy pressure for the thick strokes.

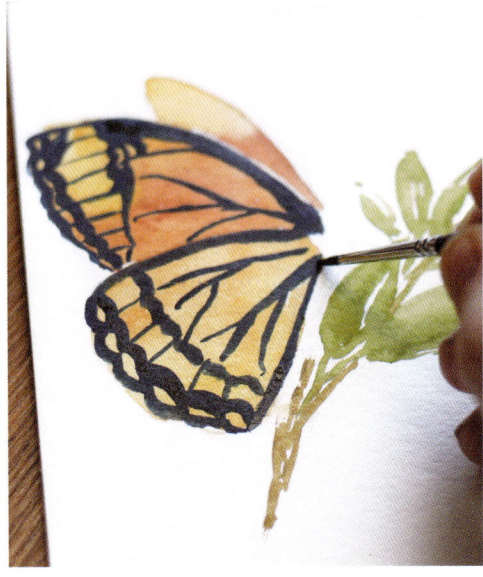

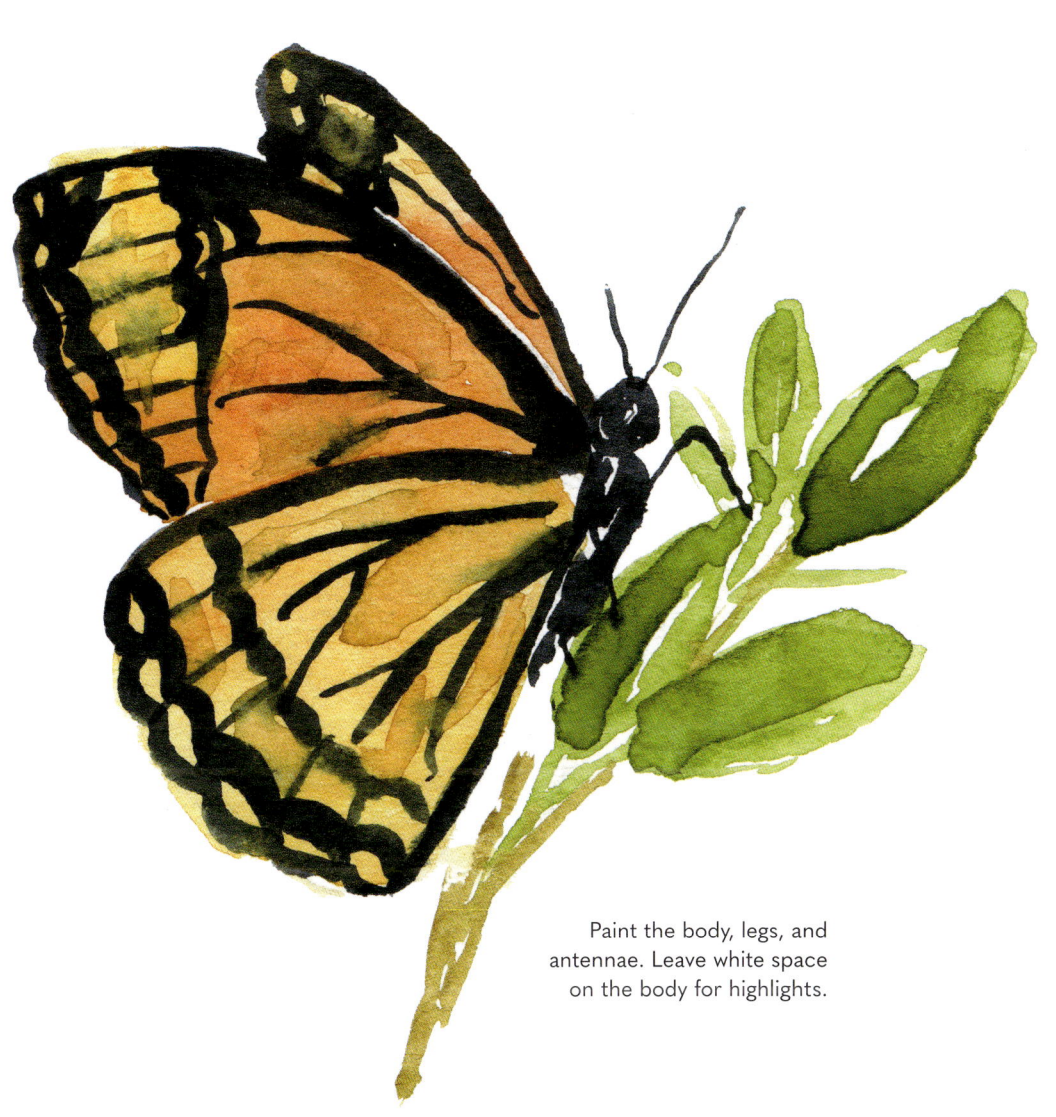

Paint the body, legs, and antennae. Leave white space on the body for highlights.

# PAINT A BEETLE

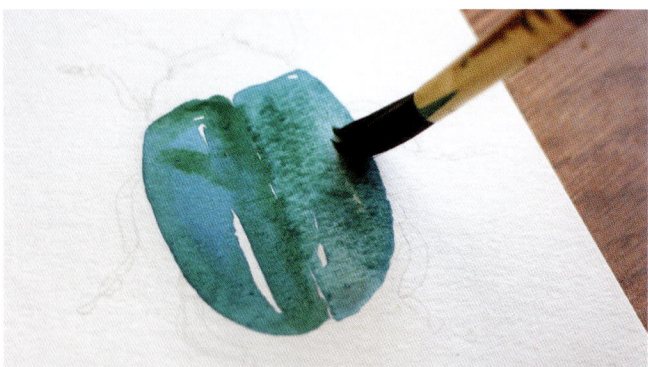

Start by painting the beetle with an even shade of blue-green paint, leaving white highlights.

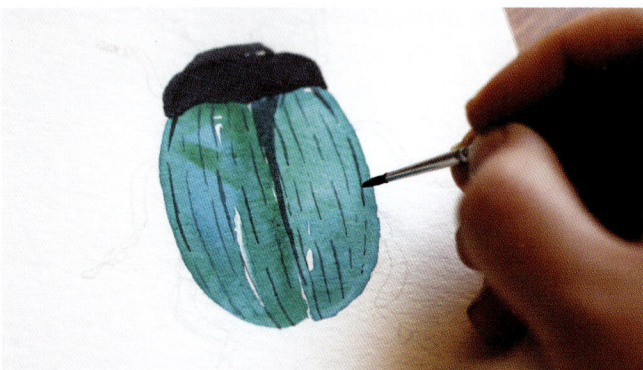

Add black to the upper sections of the beetle, bringing some of it down into the reflection on the shell. Paint thin, uneven lines on the shell to define the pattern, following the natural curve of the shell.

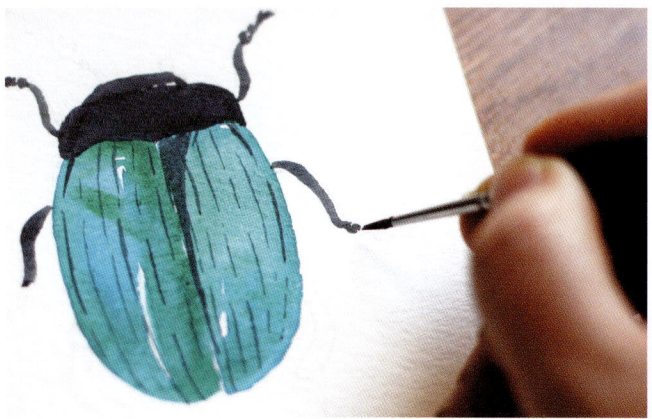

Paint the legs. Using uneven strokes on the end sections creates texture without adding too much intricate detail.

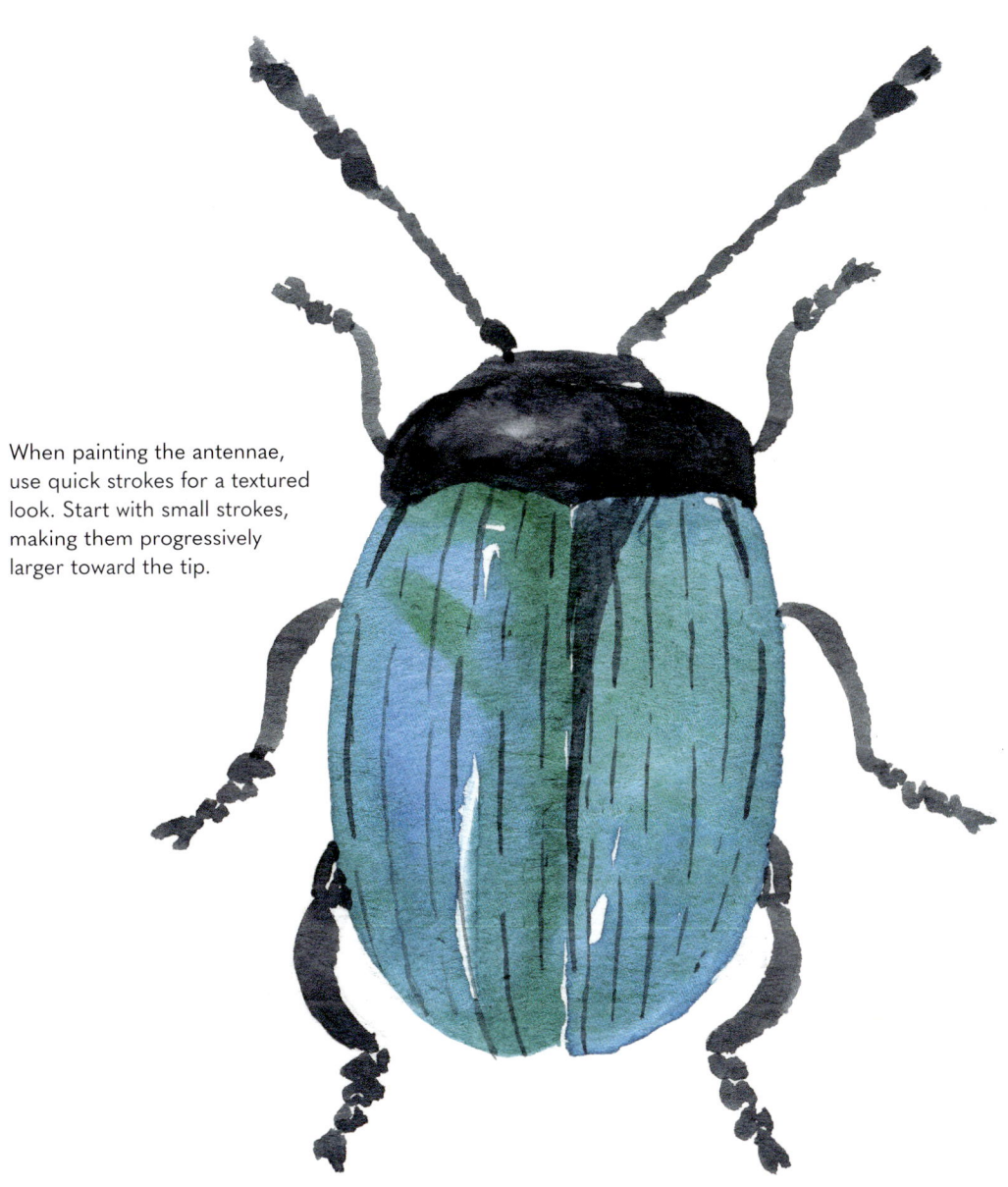

When painting the antennae, use quick strokes for a textured look. Start with small strokes, making them progressively larger toward the tip.

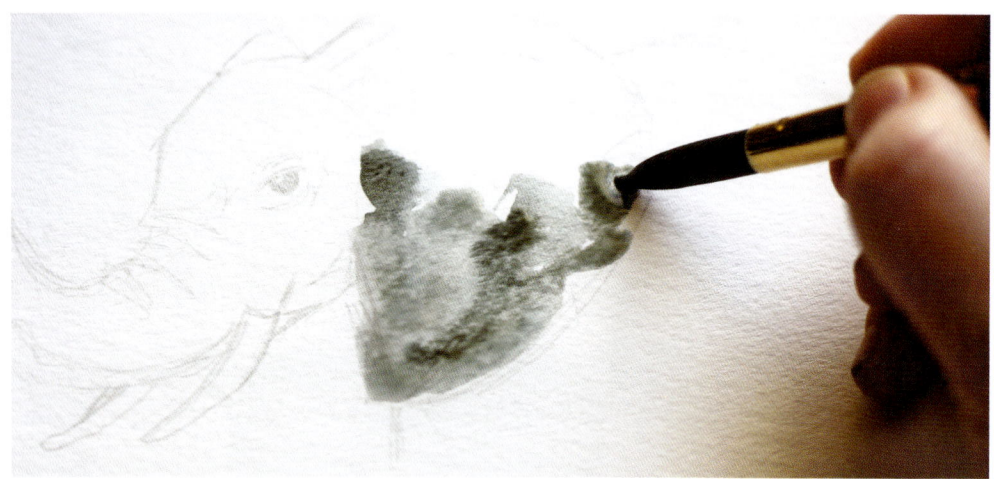

Start by painting a light gray color across the elephant's ear, leaving white space in the appropriate places, such as inside the ear, for highlights.

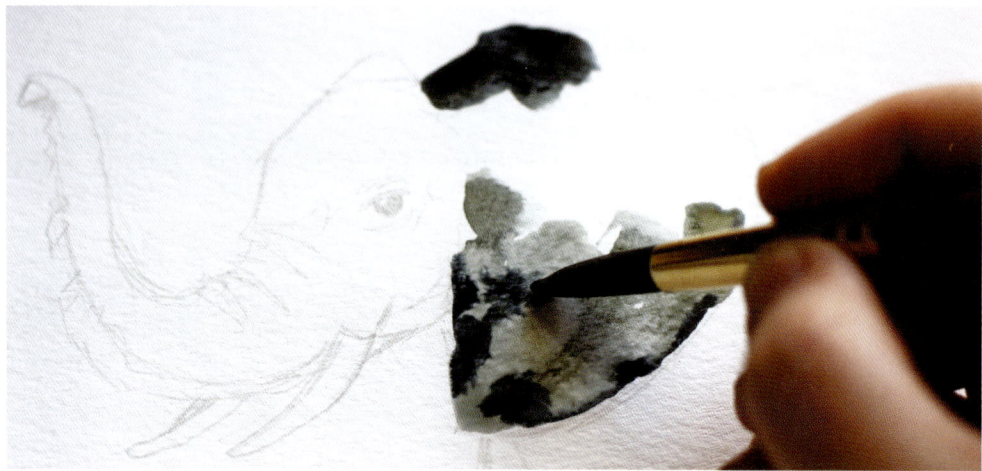

Drop in different shades of gray and blue while the paint is wet, working somewhat quickly so that an area doesn't dry before you can paint the whole section.

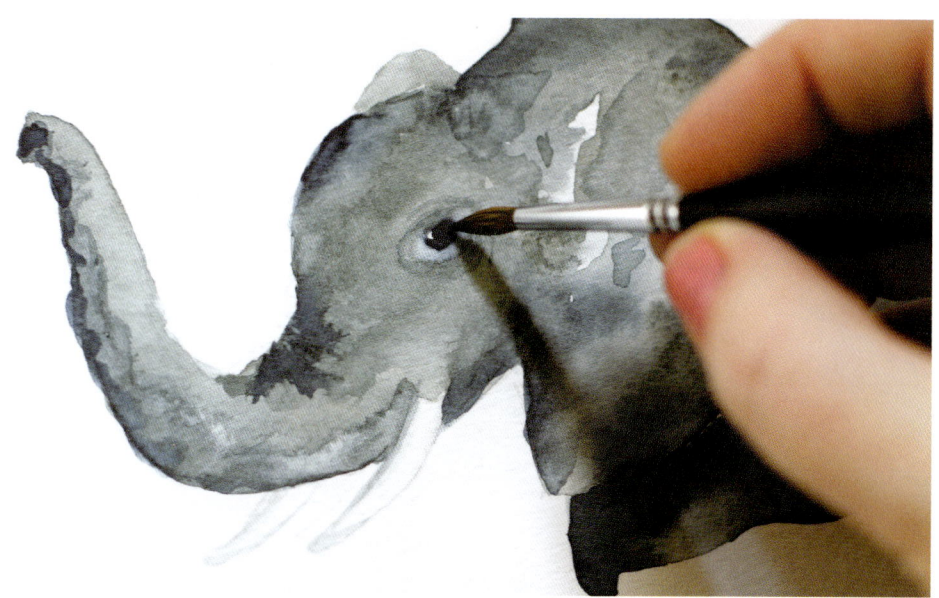

Add darker grays and blues for shadow and definition under the neck, the bottom of the trunk, and in wrinkled areas.

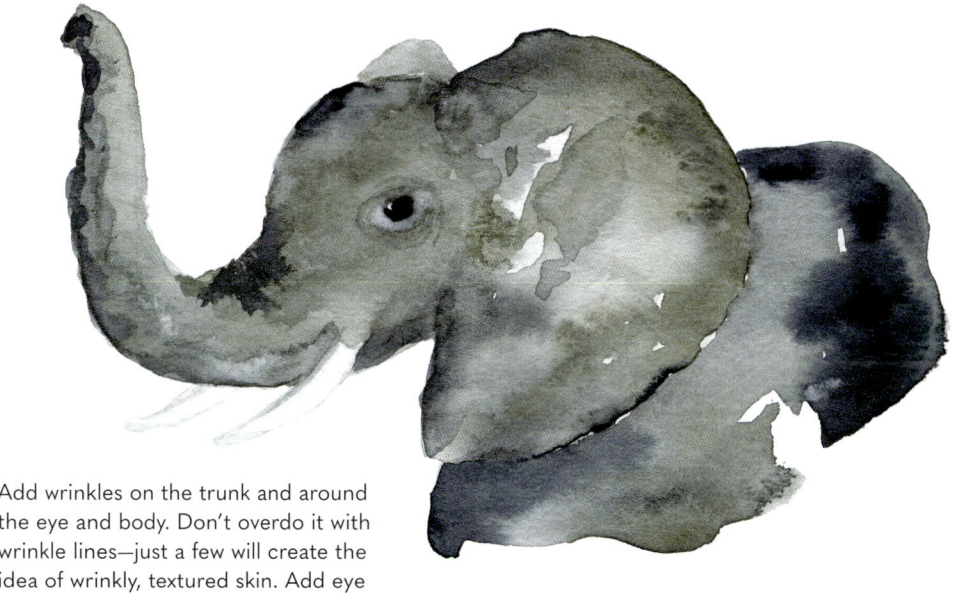

Add wrinkles on the trunk and around the eye and body. Don't overdo it with wrinkle lines—just a few will create the idea of wrinkly, textured skin. Add eye detail and shadowing under the neck and tusks.

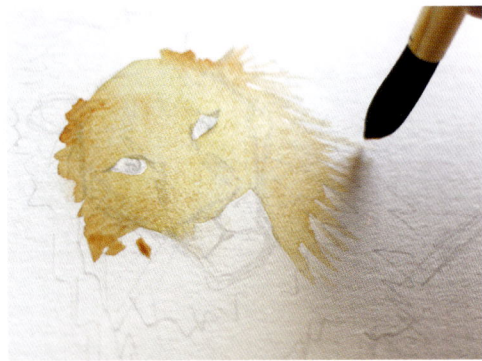

Start by painting the face light orange. Don't forget to leave the lighter areas of fur unpainted. Bring the orange paint into the mane. Make light strokes from the face outward to look like fur.

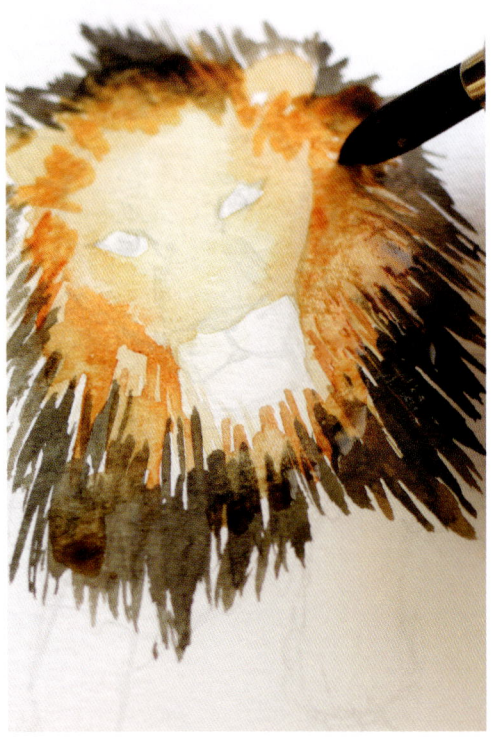

Drop in more orange paint in the mane, using a shade slightly darker than the face.

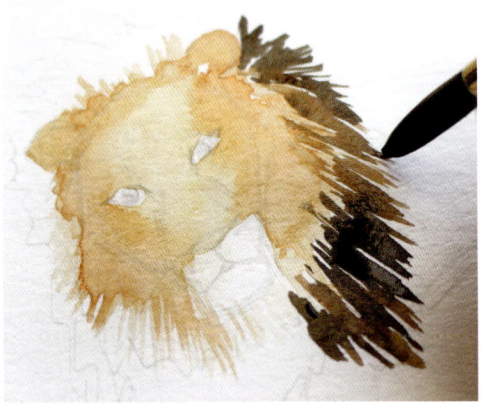

Add the dark layers of fur using chocolate brown paint. Make light strokes from just above the orange hairline growing outward. This makes it look like the orange hairs mix with the brown hairs where they meet. Leave white space for definition and highlights.

Paint the eyes, nose, and mouth. Define the ears and the hair detail around and inside them. Add light patches of brown for the texture on the lion's face and a darker brown to define the outline of the face against the mane.

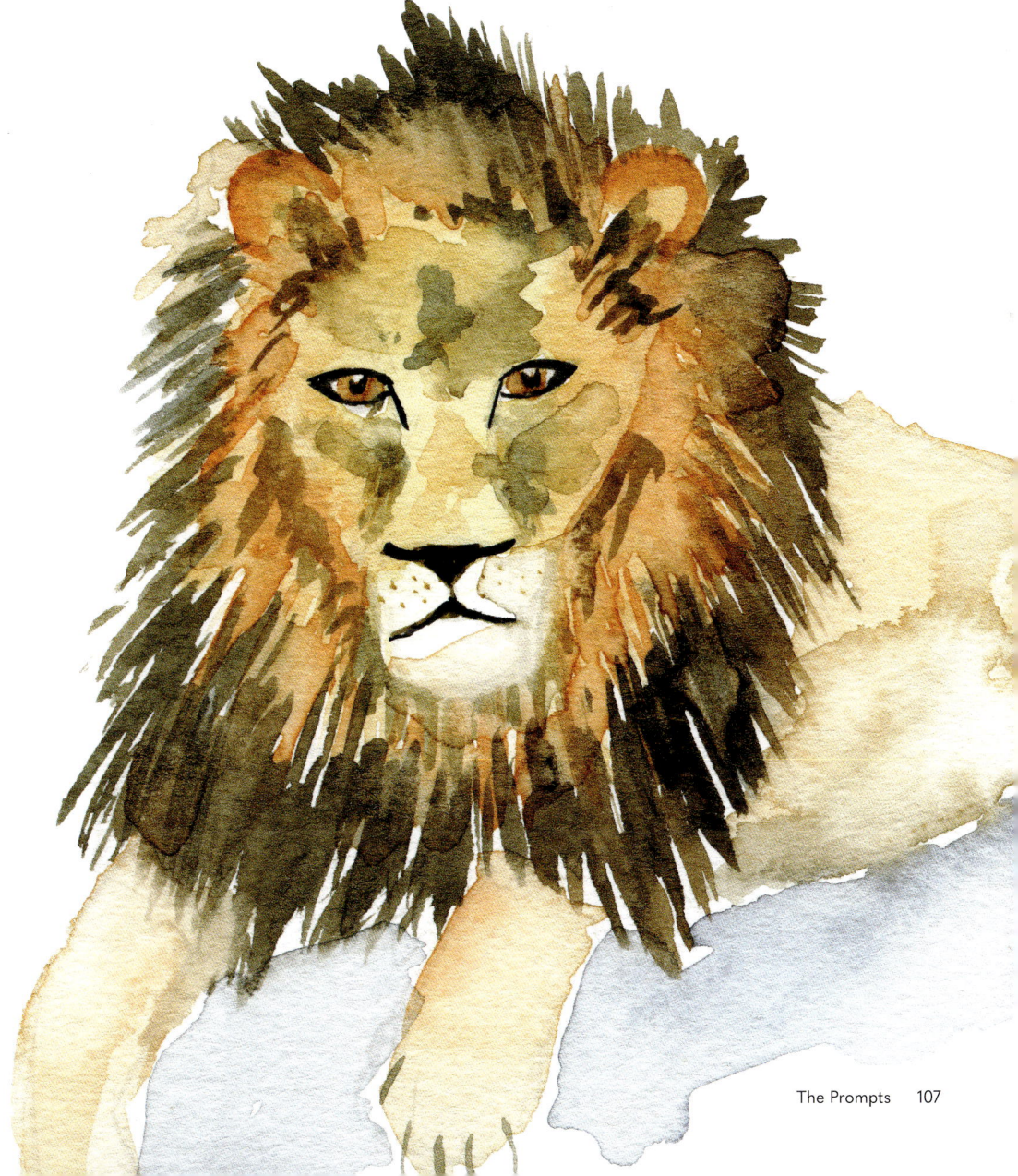

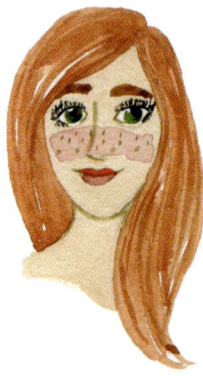

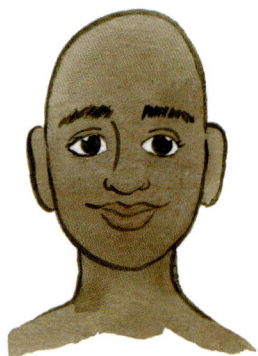

Mix pale skin colors with small amounts of yellow, red, and brown until you reach the right pigment—this face has a pink undertone.

This dark skin color mix of brown, red, and green contains a bit more red to create a reddish undertone. For a subtle, natural effect, opt for a very light lip color. For bald heads, be sure to define the shape of the head proportionally.

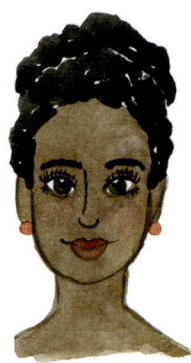

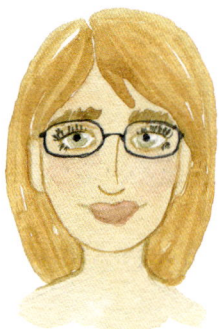

Mix dark skin colors with brown, red, and green. The green helps balance the mix so that it isn't too red. For thick, curly hair like this, leave sporadic areas of white space to define the curls.

To create a pale skin tone that has a golden undertone, combine yellow, red, and brown, but use more yellow.

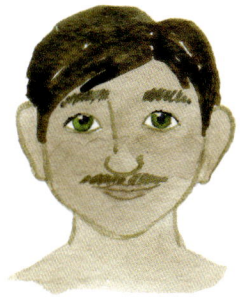

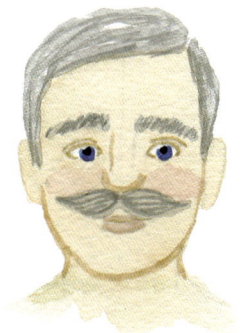

Like pale skin tones, light brown or tan skin is also a mix of yellow, red, and brown. Add small amounts of paint until you reach the right pigment. The yellow paint will help prevent the color from getting too dark.

To create a pale skin color mix, combine yellow, red, and brown as usual, but make the mixture very watered down.

## 57 PAINT A SELF-PORTRAIT

*Painting portraits can be challenging, but it's possible to create whimsical faces that capture the person's essence. Just like with animals, a few well-placed strokes and details go a long way. Review these examples and follow the tips as you practice painting your own face!*

*To paint this pretty lakeside scene, start by brushing plain water over the entire sheet of watercolor paper. While the paper is wet, add drops of yellow and blue watercolor randomly across the surface. Be sure to leave some white space. Allow the colors to bleed together.*

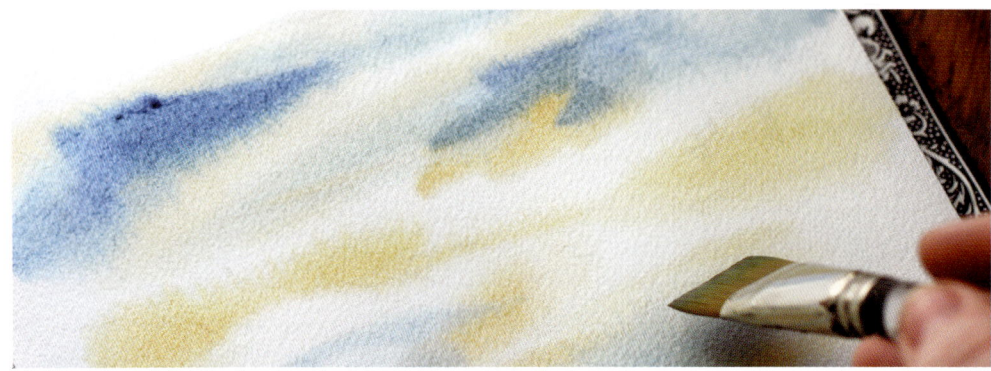

To paint this pretty lakeside scene, start by brushing plain water over the entire sheet of watercolor paper. While the paper is wet, add drops of yellow and blue watercolor randomly across the surface. Be sure to leave some white space. Allow the colors to bleed together.

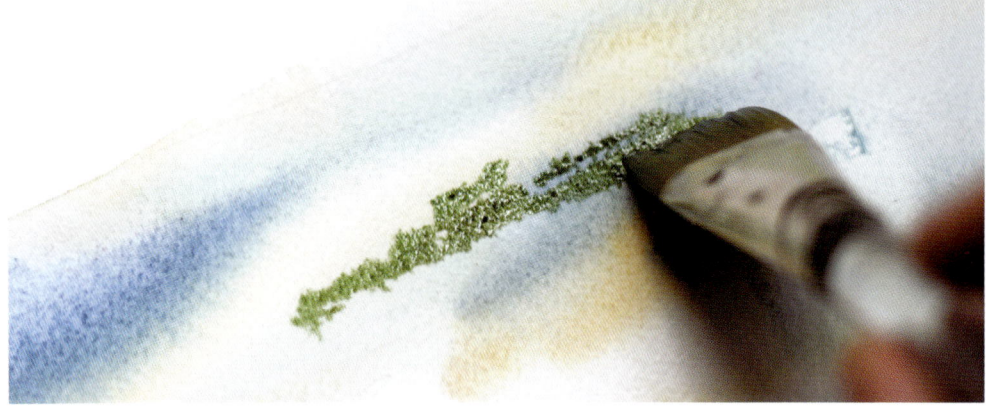

Allow the paint and paper to dry. Then start dabbing green watercolor paint along the horizon line.

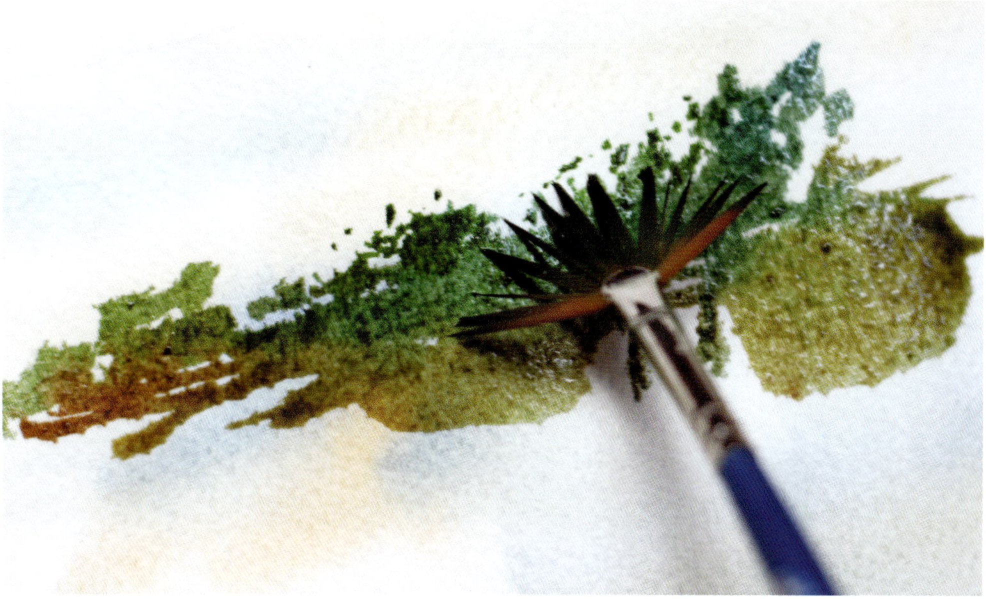

Begin adding multiple shades of green and other colors to create a natural, interesting appearance. Use a fan brush to create texture and give the impression of leafy bushes and trees.

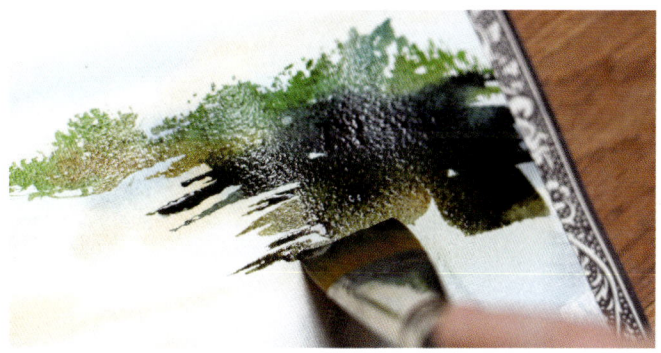

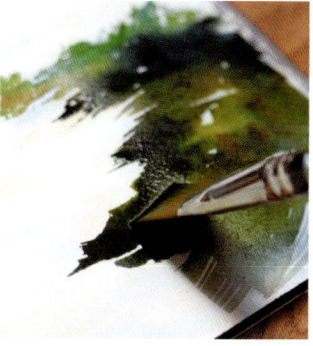

Bring color down along the side of the page to create the shoreline. Use light horizontal strokes, pulling into what will be the water. This will give the impression that the land juts into the lake and isn't an even, perfect border.

Continue to sweep color along the page, using a variety of earthy, natural colors.

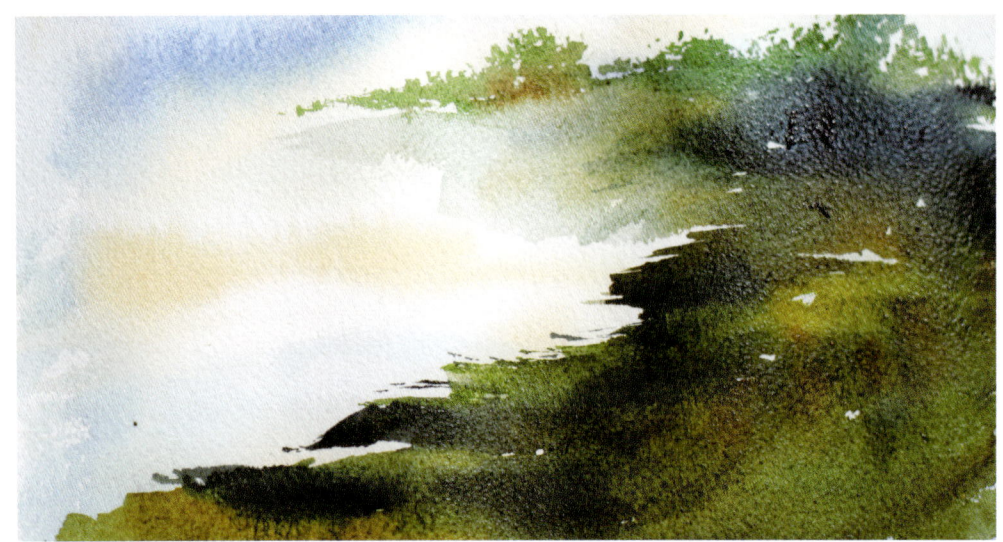

When you reach the edge of the desired shoreline on the other side of the page, stop and look over your work to ensure you've added all the colors you want before the paint dries. Here, you can see how I blended some of the colors at the top beyond the waterline to create blurred shadows in the water.

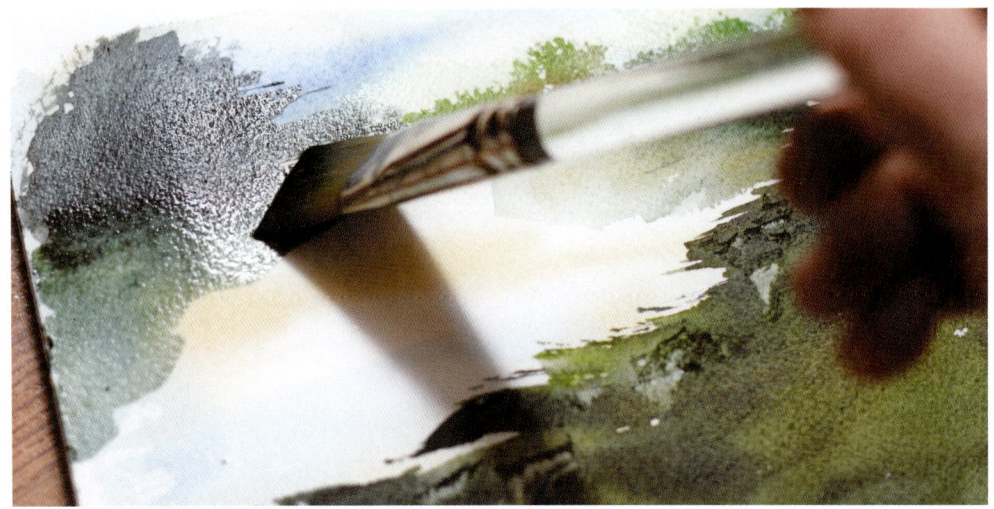

Add the other shoreline, creating texture and the impression of large trees.

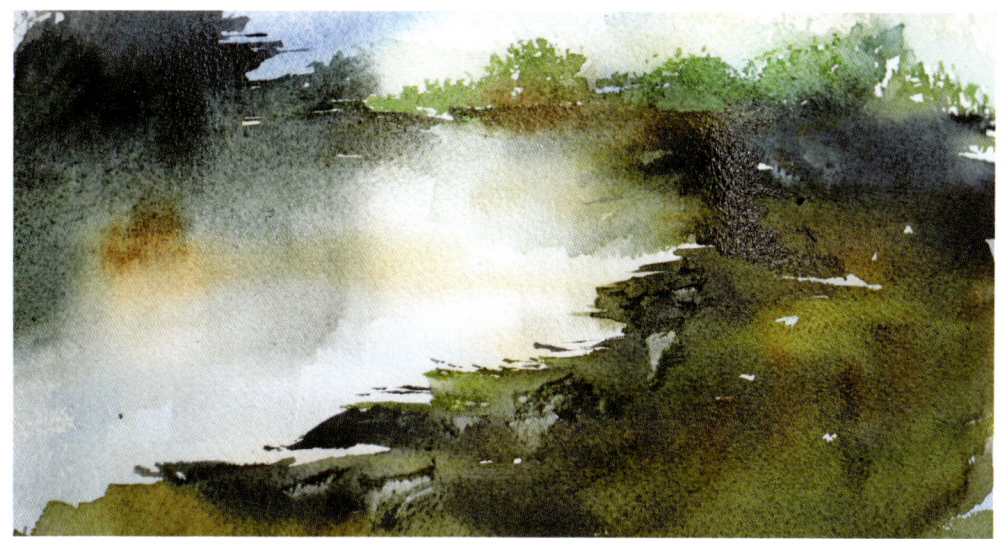

Dampen your brush with water and pull down some of the colors into the water to create reflected shadows.

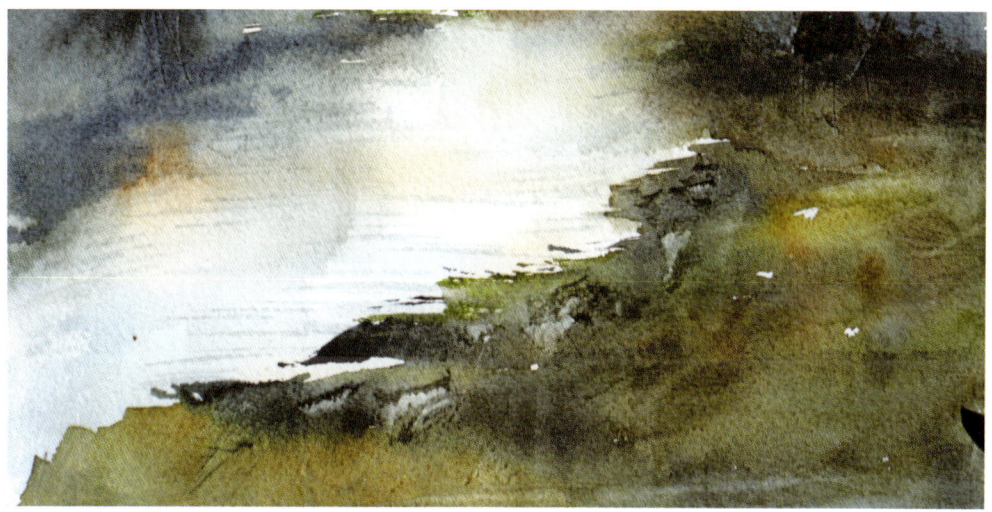

Add light horizontal lines along the water to create movement and texture. Add any finishing details to complete the piece.

PAINT A TWILIGHT LANDSCAPE

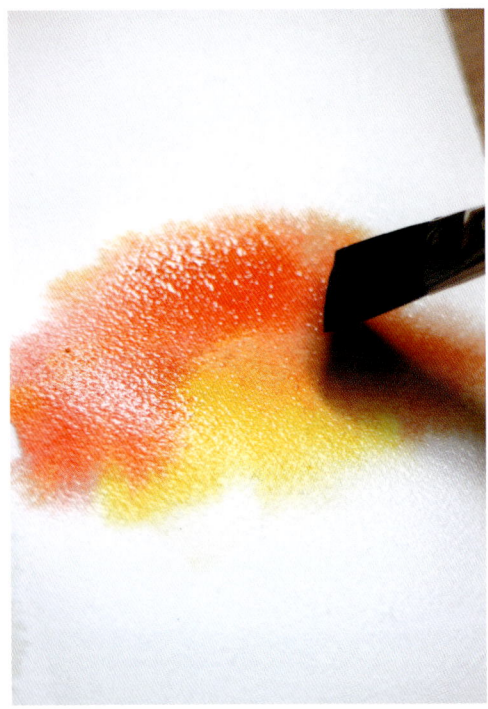 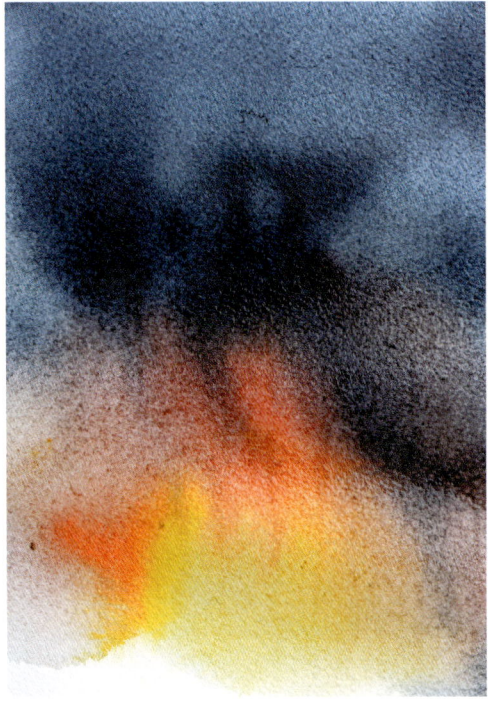

Paint the upper two-thirds of the paper with plain water. Then, apply a highly concentrated area of bright yellow watercolor paint on the lower end of the wet section of paper. Apply reds and oranges at the top of and around the yellow paint, allowing the colors to blend.

Add dark blues, blacks, and purples at and above the red and orange paint. Allow the colors to softly blend while still maintaining the red color.

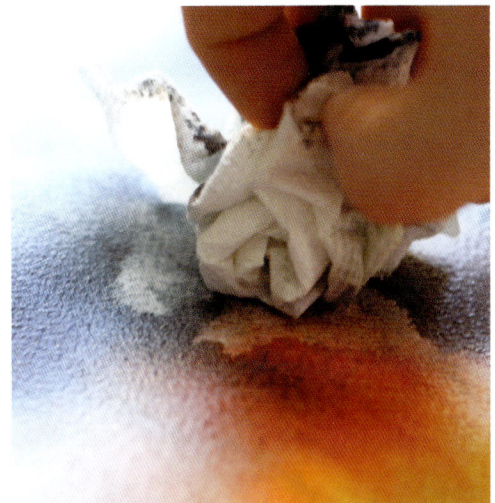

Before the paper dries completely, lightly dab some of the paint away with a paper towel to create texture and movement in the night sky. If needed, you can apply diluted paint over the dabbed areas to bring back a little more color.

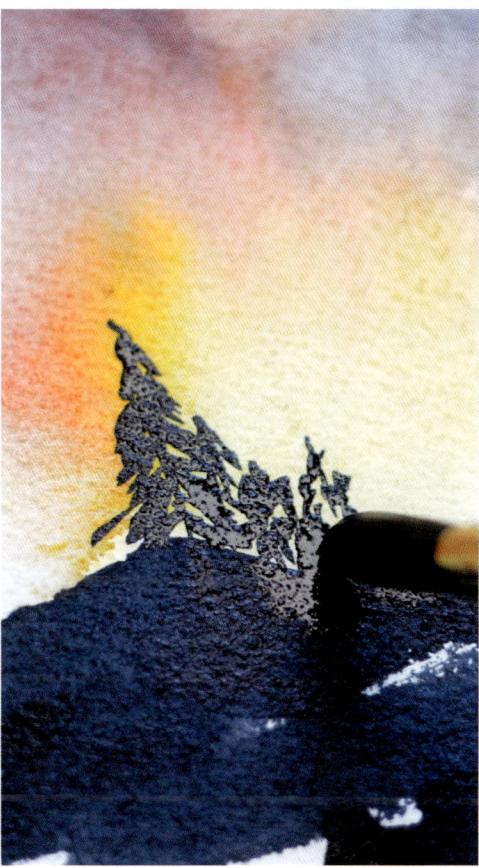

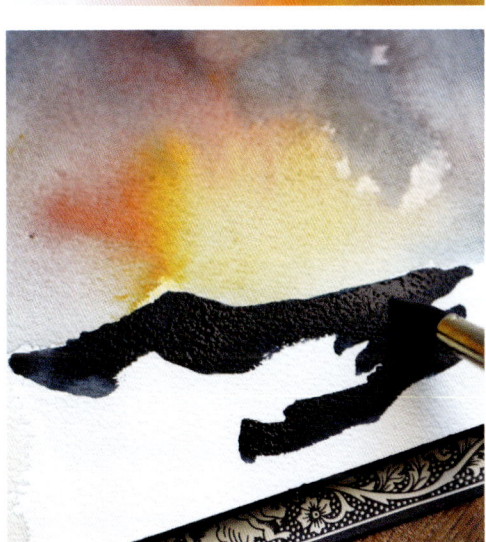

Allow the paint to dry completely. Then, begin painting the horizon using dark blue and black paints.

Begin to add mountains and trees against the colorful sky.

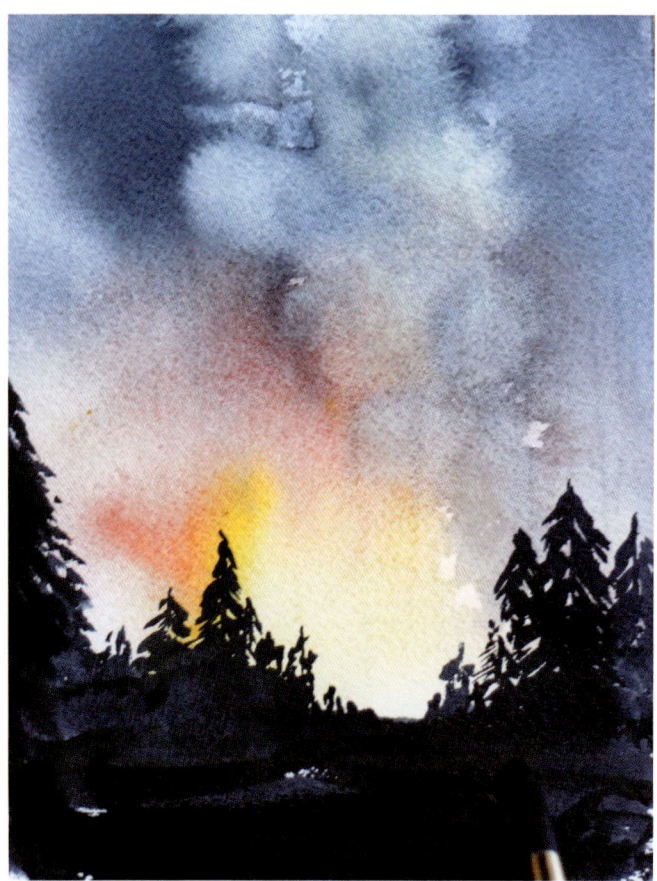

As you paint the trees, keep in mind that they should be more textured at the outer branches and very dense near the trunk. Paint the trees at different sizes to create depth.

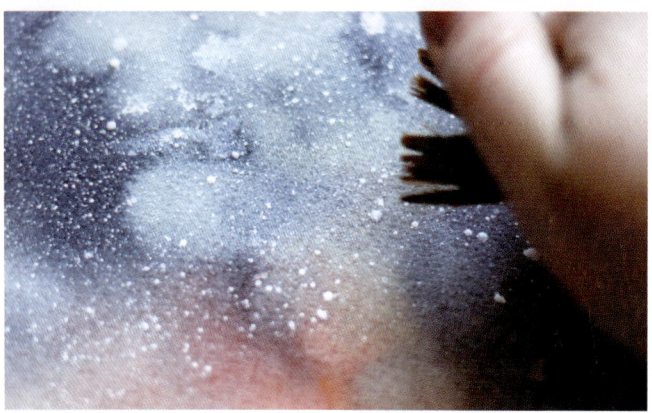

To create stars, dip a flat brush or toothbrush into white ink. Flick the ink onto the paper using your thumb. Be sure to cover the dark trees with paper to keep them free of white dots!

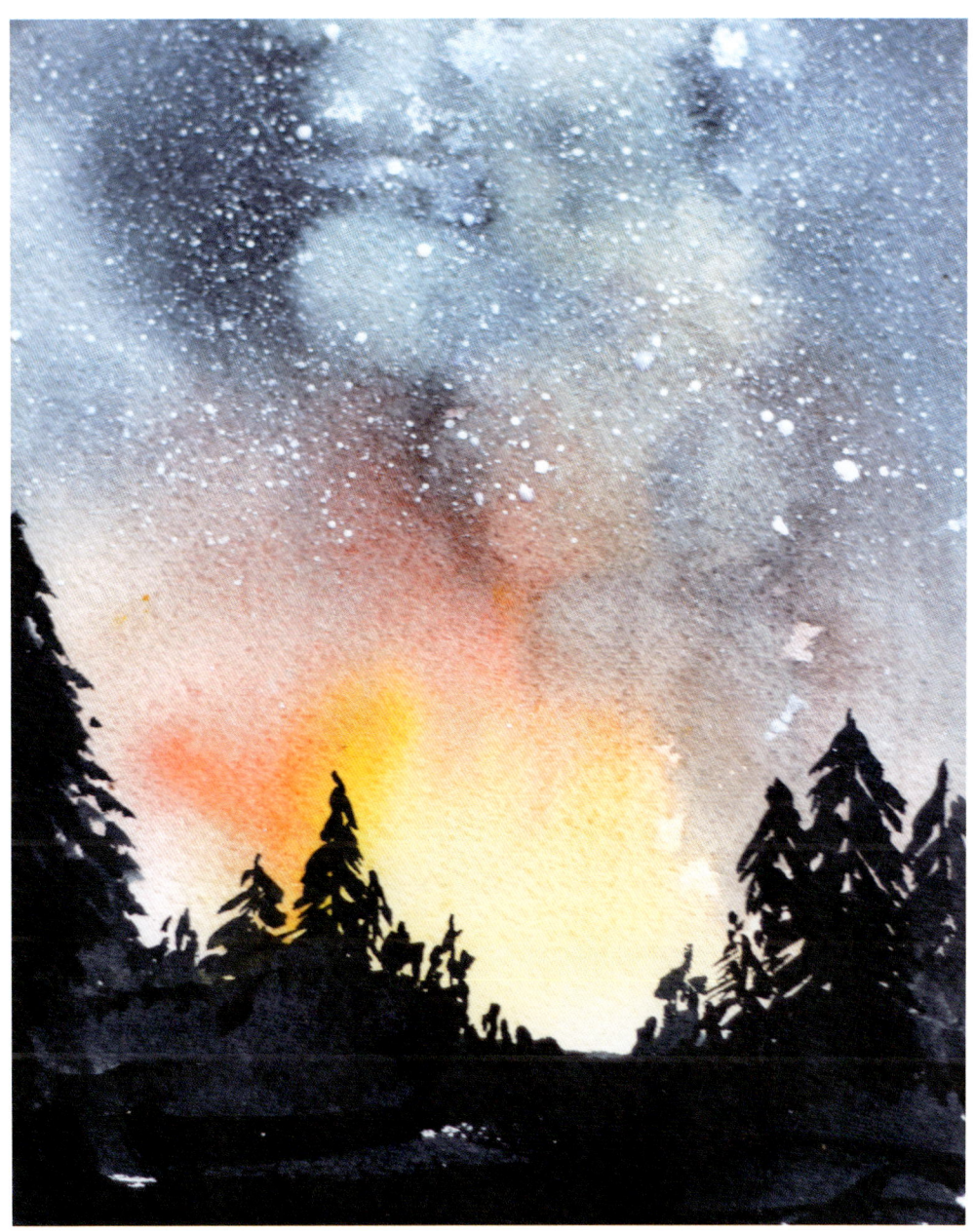

You can use these simple steps and techniques to paint endless beautiful sunset scenes.

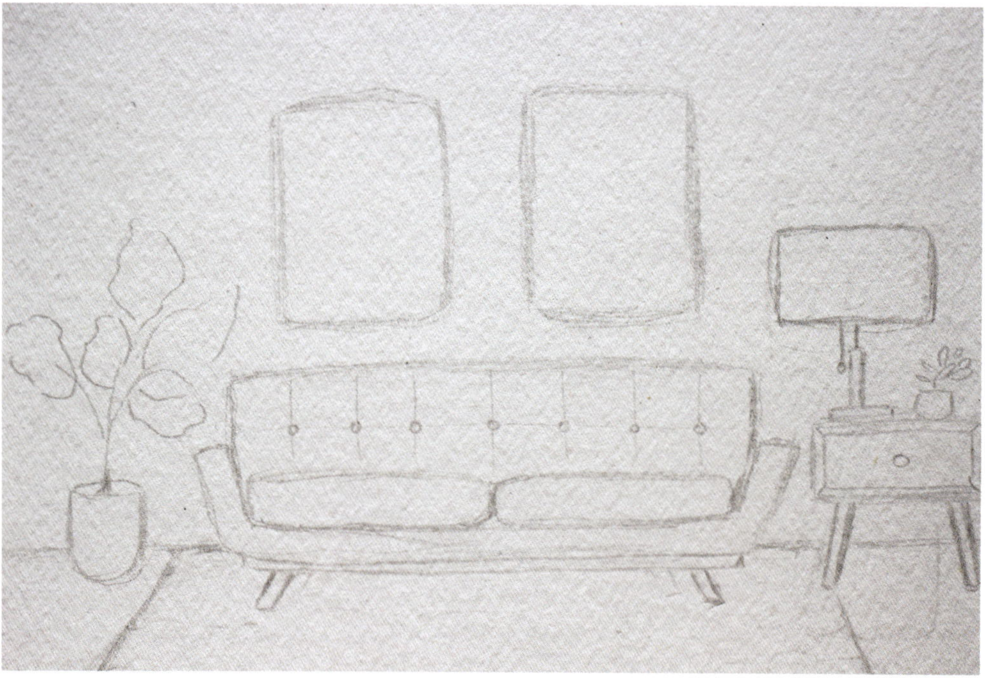

Start by planning the interior with a sketch to ensure the proportions and perspective are accurate.

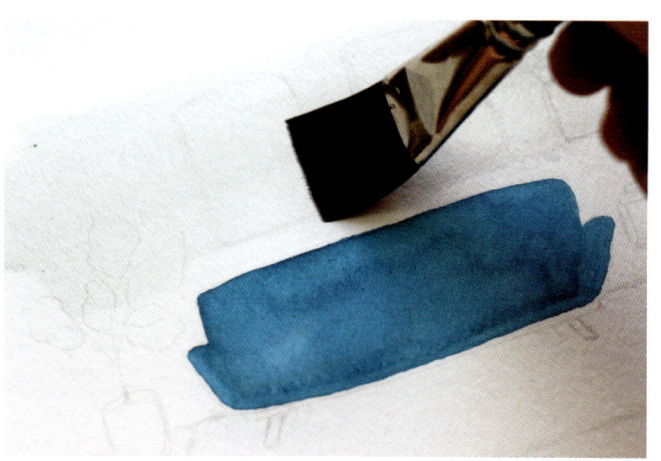

Begin painting the objects in the room with a flat base of color. I started with the blue couch. For this room, I wanted a light gray wall, so I painted that before moving on to the other elements.

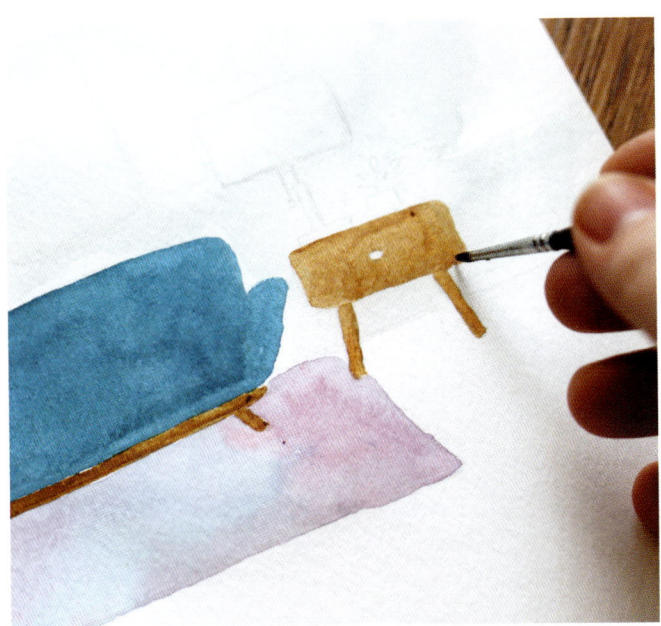

Continue painting the other objects in the room. As you work, allow areas of paint to dry before painting other parts that touch to avoid blending colors. For example, let the paint on the couch dry before painting the wood frame and legs. For the rug, I blended multiple colors together for a vintage look.

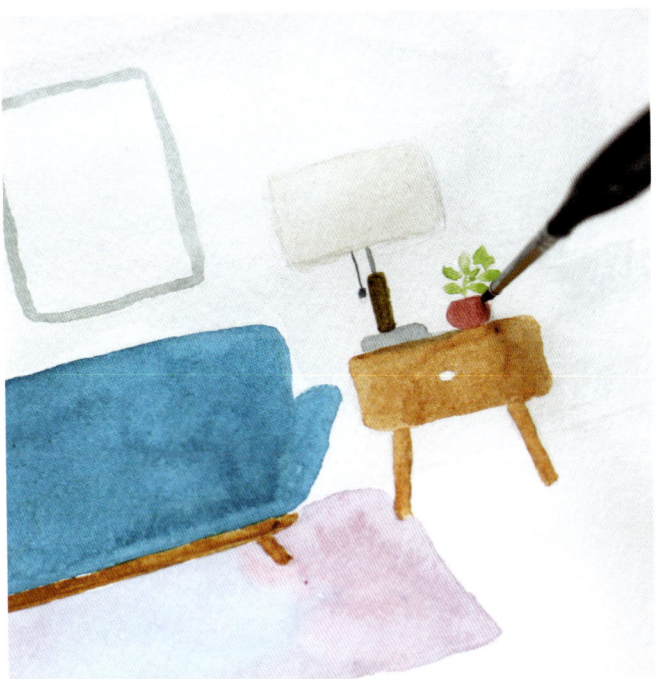

Begin painting a base color on all the smaller objects in the room, such as the lamp. Then add plants and greenery—my favorite part!

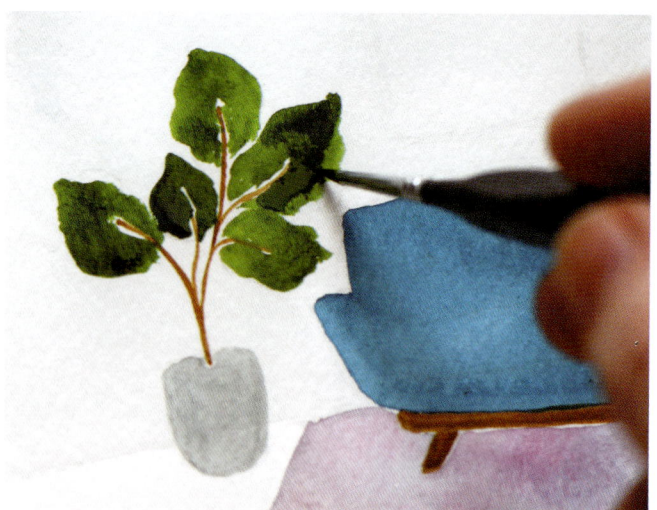

You can refer to the prompts on painting botanicals for tips on painting the greenery and flowers.

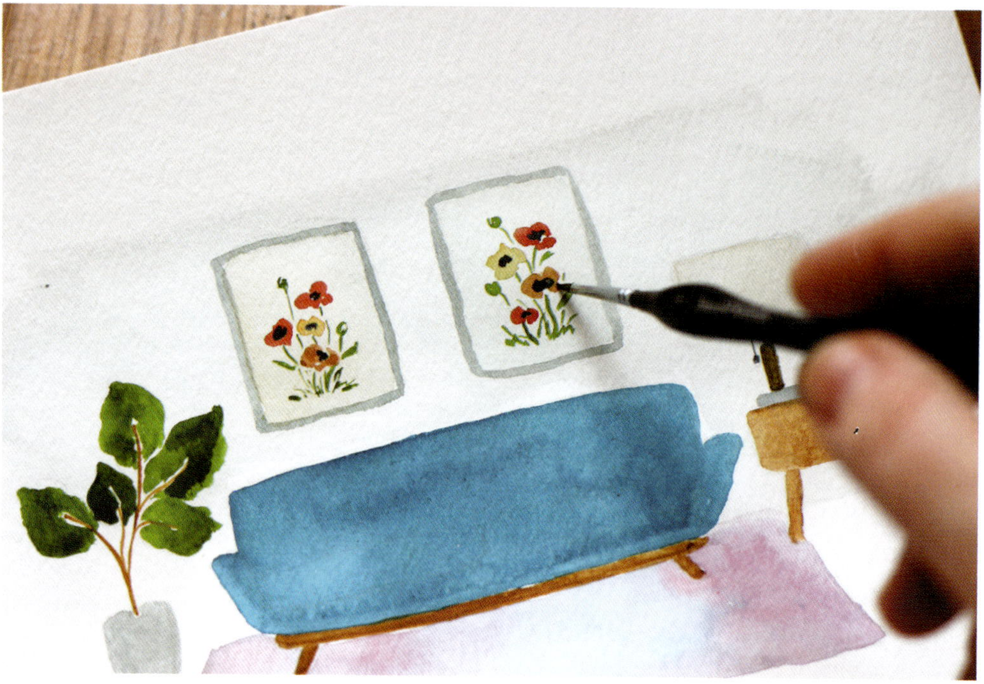

Create artwork for the wall.

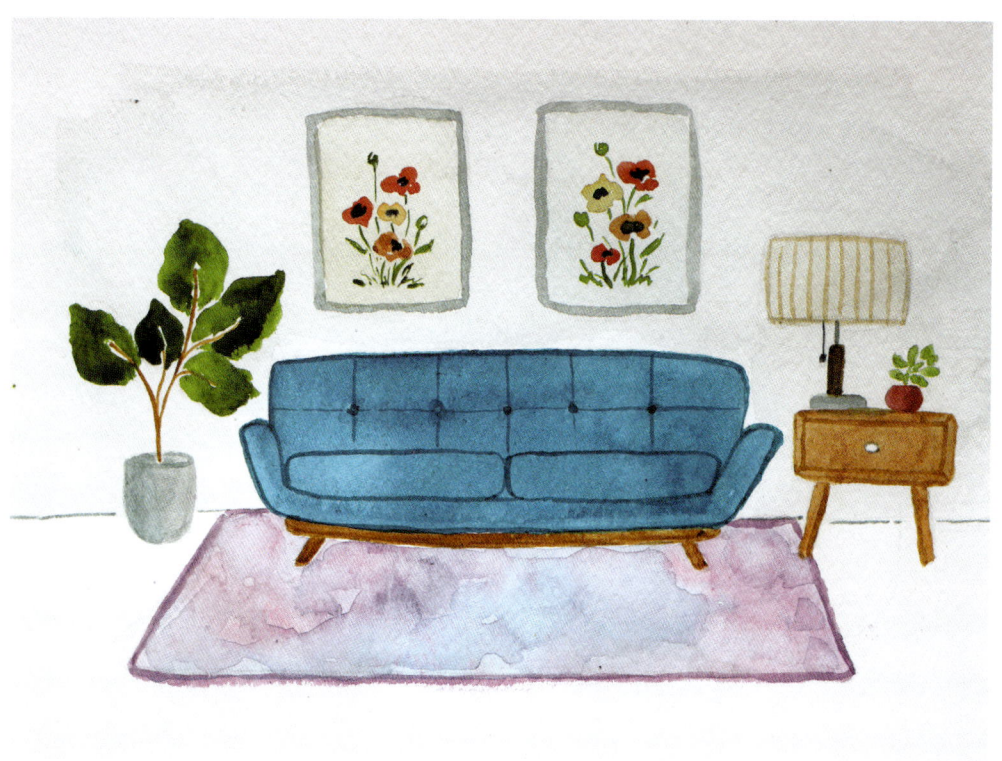

Finish with details, such as lines and buttons on the couch for the tufting.

# 61    PAINT A COZY COTTAGE

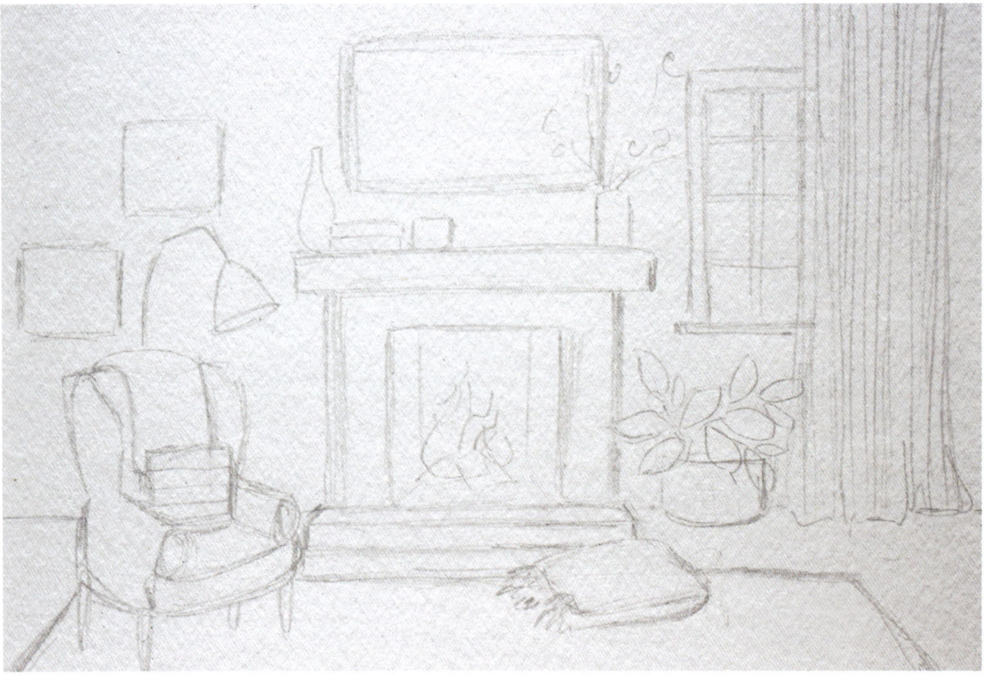

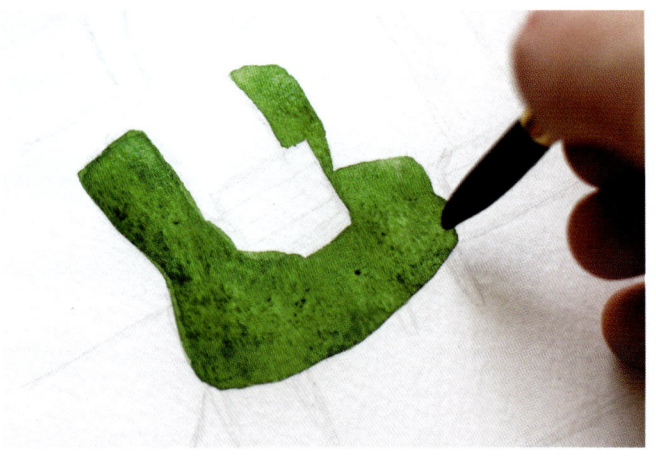

Begin with a detailed sketch of the room.

Paint a base layer of color on the chair and let it dry.

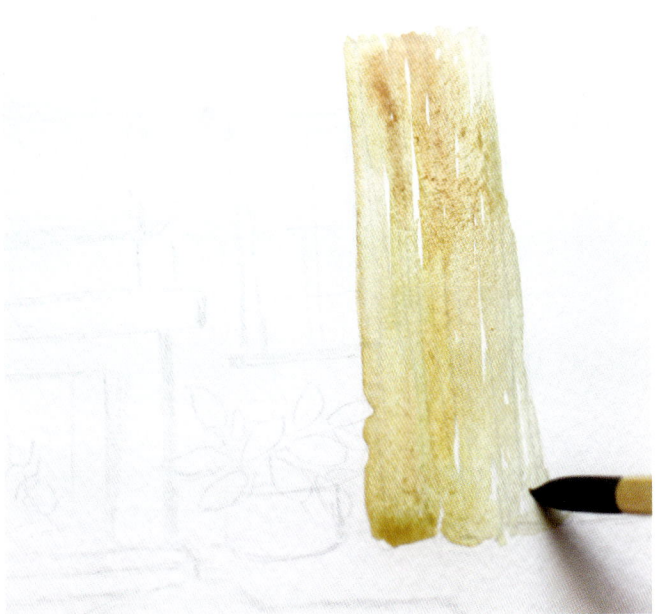

Paint the curtains with a light base color, leaving white space for highlights and definition.

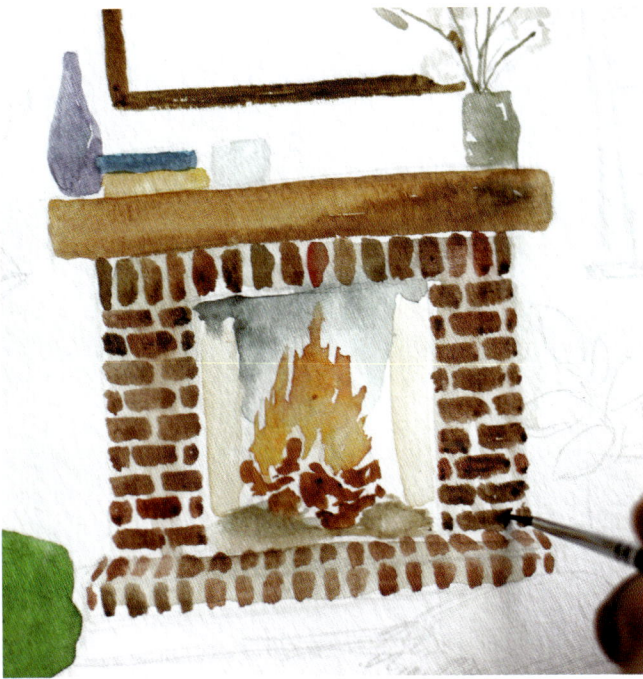

Add color to the mantle and smaller objects on top. Then, paint the bricks on the fireplace. To create a natural look for the brick, vary the paint color slightly and make some strokes shorter on the edges to indicate smaller bricks. Paint the fire inside.

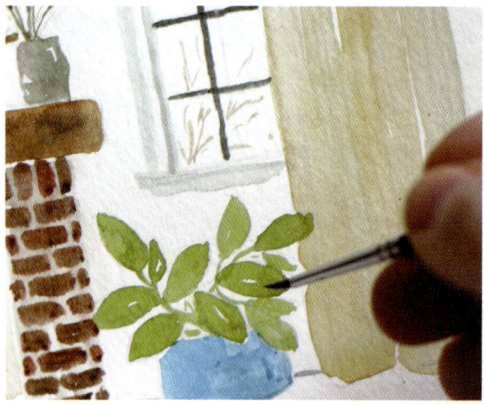

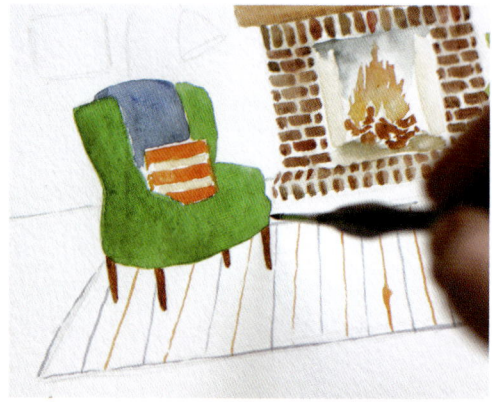

Paint the plant and its container and add detail to the window and a branch outside.

Paint the chair legs, pillow, and blanket to add more color. Add stripes to the rug.

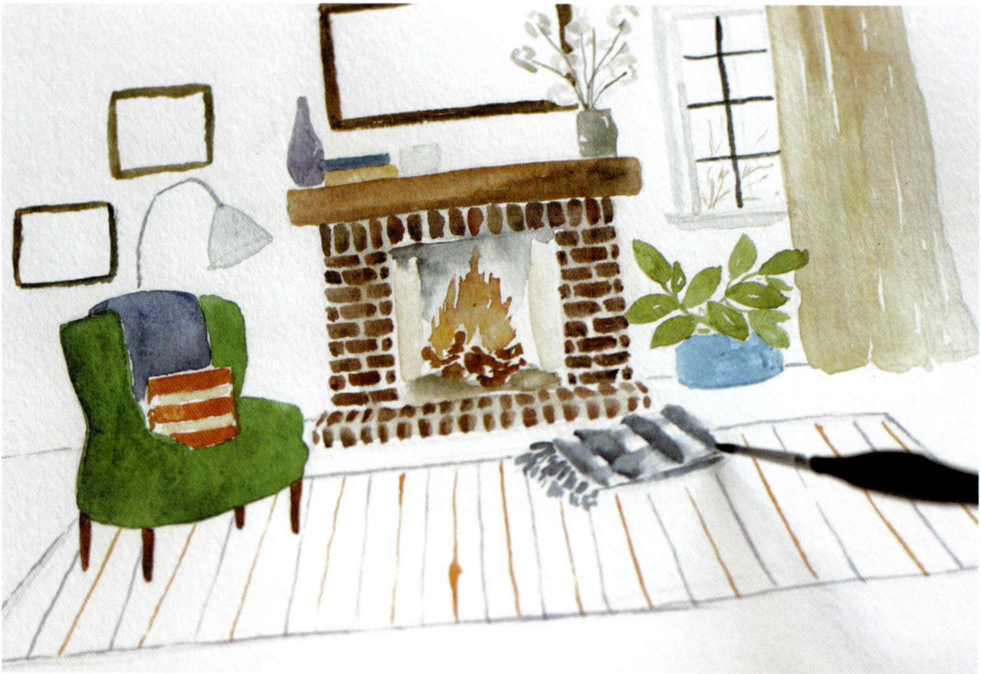

Paint the floor blanket, the lamp, and the frames on the wall.

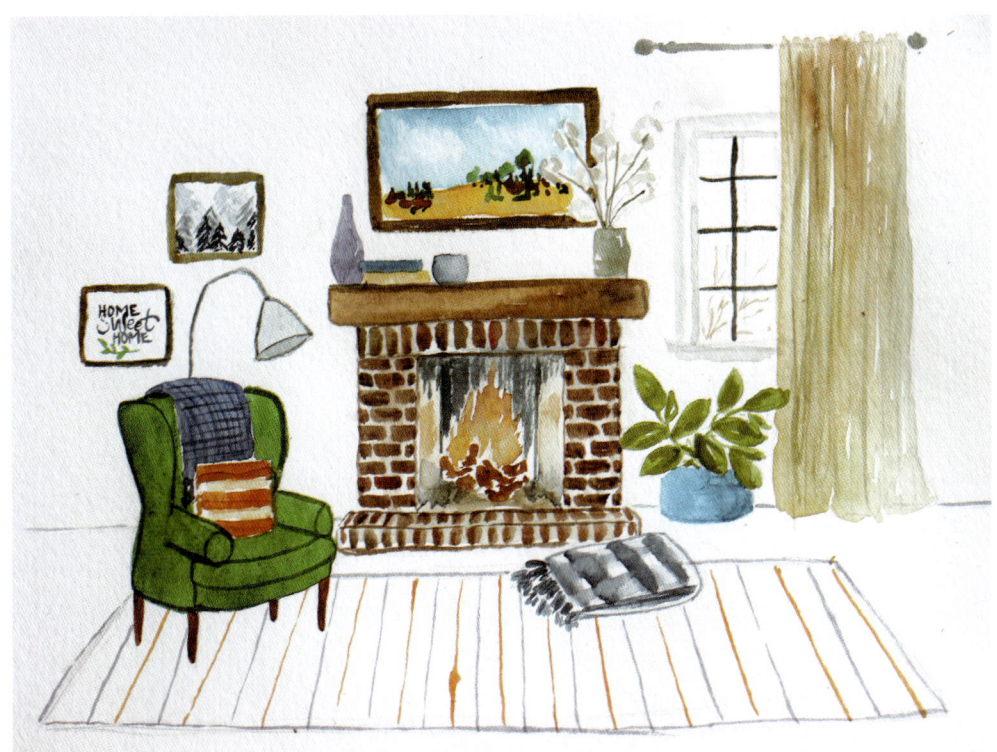

Add all the finishing details, including the lines on the plaid blanket, a dark outline on the chair and floor lamp, and some darker strokes in the curtain and plant leaves to add dimension. Don't forget to add artwork to the frames. Do any of these pieces look familiar?

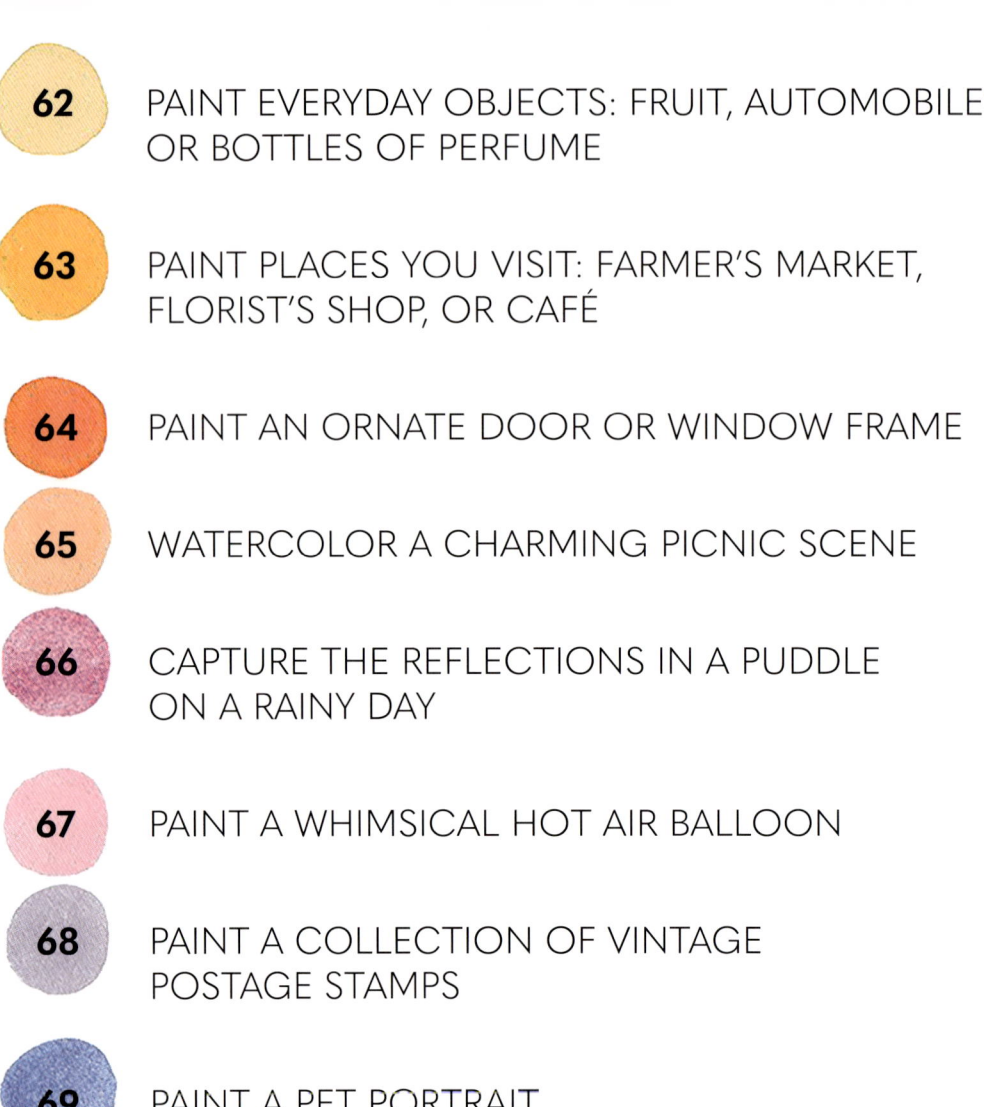

**62** PAINT EVERYDAY OBJECTS: FRUIT, AUTOMOBILES, OR BOTTLES OF PERFUME

**63** PAINT PLACES YOU VISIT: FARMER'S MARKET, FLORIST'S SHOP, OR CAFÉ

**64** PAINT AN ORNATE DOOR OR WINDOW FRAME

**65** WATERCOLOR A CHARMING PICNIC SCENE

**66** CAPTURE THE REFLECTIONS IN A PUDDLE ON A RAINY DAY

**67** PAINT A WHIMSICAL HOT AIR BALLOON

**68** PAINT A COLLECTION OF VINTAGE POSTAGE STAMPS

**69** PAINT A PET PORTRAIT

**70** CREATE YOUR OWN PROMPTS

*The prompts don't stop here! Let your imagination run, and jot down your own ideas.*

Kristin Van Leuven is a watercolor artist best known for her loose style and modern approach to painting. After trying different mediums, watercolor quickly became her favorite because of its unpredictable nature and blending ability. An Arizona native, she is inspired by nature and the beautiful desert around her. After many years of painting, she was encouraged by her family to post her work on social media, where she found a supportive community that has helped her artwork and business succeed. She is blessed with a loving husband and three beautiful children. When she isn't busy with family and artwork, she loves to read books and be outside with her family. Visit www.lovelypeople. bigcartel.com to see more of Kristin's artwork.

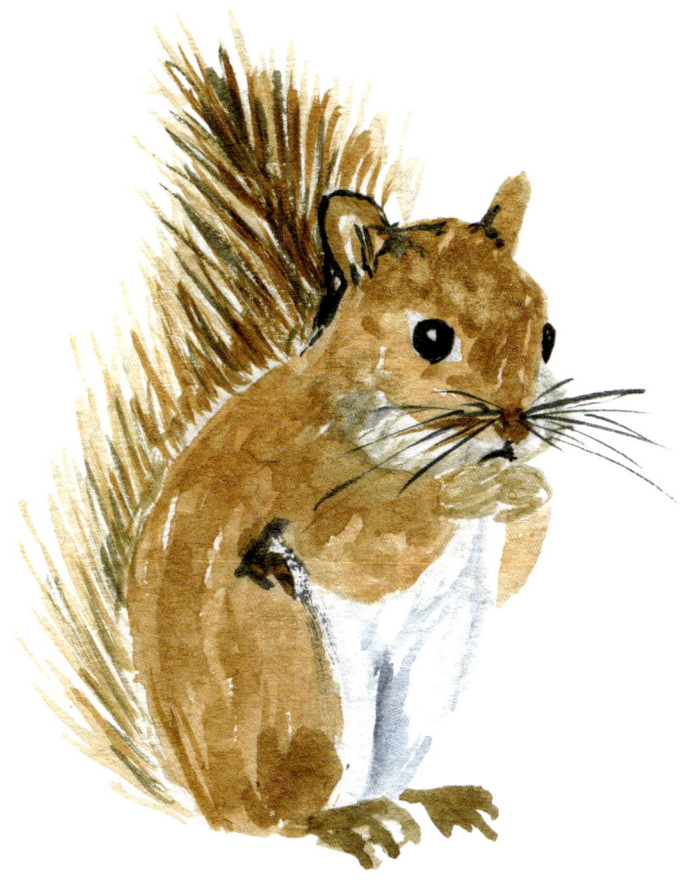

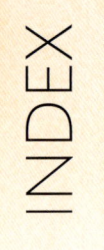

# INDEX